ULTIMATE

PERSONAL BRAND CHECKLIST

DR. JEROME JOSEPH

GLOBAL BRAND THOUGHT LEADER

notionpress.com

INDIA • SINGAPORE • MALAYSIA

ISBN 979-8-89233-923-0

CONTENTS

- Social Proof Points: Testimonials
- Social Proof Points: Media Features/Awards
- Social Proof Points: Credibility
- Social Proof Points: Thought Leadership
- Social Proof Points: Network Influence

CHAPTER 6 DELIVER

- Visual Branding
- The Psychology of Colour
- Brand Assets
- Online Presence
- Content Strategy
- Social Media
- Community Creation & Engagement
- Video Marketing
- LinkedIn Mastery
- Lead Generation
- Career Brand Visibility
- Pitching Your Personal Brand
- Controversial Branding
- Going Viral
- Offline Visibility
- Brand Experience
- Neuroscience & Branding

CHAPTER 7 DRIVE

- Strategic Brand Communication: Action Plan
- Multi-Funnel Approach for Personal Branding
- AI and Personal Branding
- TOP AI tools to Consider
- Online Brand Ecosystem
- Transparency, Intimacy & Reliability
- Corporate Social Responsibility
- Brand Performance Monitoring and Analytics
- Professional & Personal Development
- Financial & Legal Brand Assessment
- Work-Life Balance
- Global Reach
- Brand Extensions
- Retrospective and Future Planning
- Exit Strategies and Succession Planning
- Brand Crisis Communication

CHAPTER 1

INTRODUCTION

The Changing Landscape of Personal Branding

The 21st century has witnessed a seismic shift in how brands are built and perceived, primarily due to technological advancements and a more interconnected global community. As personal branding continues gaining momentum, conducting periodic audits of your brand's health is becoming increasingly essential. In this climate, your personal brand isn't just your business card; it's your identity, reputation, and ticket to professional growth and personal fulfilment.

For over 27 years, I've worked with over a thousand clients in over 37 countries. From Silicon Valley start-ups to Asian multinationals, from Europe to Africa, the one common denominator has been the profound impact of effective personal branding. The challenges, although varying in scale and scope, often resonate universally. These experiences have enriched this checklist, infusing it with real-world insights.

Whether coaching a fledgling entrepreneur or a C-suite executive, breakthroughs have often been catalysed by a well-structured brand audit. I have seen personal brands rise from obscurity to prominence, and professionals elevate their careers merely by systematically addressing and implementing the points in checklists similar to the ones you're about to delve into.

Why Personal Branding Matters More Than Ever

In an era where we all have a digital footprint, personal branding is not a luxury- it's a necessity. The rise of social media, the gig economy, and remote work has made your personal brand an extension of yourself, public and ever-present. Gone are the days when branding was solely for corporations with deep pockets. Today, individual entrepreneurs, freelancers, and professionals must also be adept marketers of their most valuable product: themselves.

The Necessity of this Checklist

CLARITY
Having a structured checklist brings highlights to your personal brand's most vital components, ensuring everything is noticed.

EFFICIENCY
Checklists provide a roadmap for branding efforts, allowing you to allocate time and resources more effectively.

ACCOUNTABILITY
Checklists act as your auditor, tracking your personal brand's health metrics and keeping you committed to your brand vision.

ADAPTABILITY
Markets change, trends come and go, and career circumstances shift. A checklist helps you keep tabs, adapt, and grow with these changes, ensuring your brand remains relevant.

How to Use this Checklist

INITIAL REVIEW
Start with the overview, marking each section as completed. Not every section may apply to you yet, so skip the ones that are not relevant.

EFFICIENCY
For those areas that are still in progress or untouched, you can probe deeper to uncover deficiencies, and you might find the need to fill it out in the future.

ACCOUNTABILITY
Checklists act as your auditor, tracking your personal brand's health metrics and keeping you committed to your brand vision.

ADAPTABILITY
Markets change, trends come and go, and career circumstances shift. A checklist helps you keep tabs, adapt, and grow with these changes, ensuring your brand remains relevant.

CHAPTER 2

HOW TO NAVIGATE THIS BOOK: A GUIDE THROUGH THE 5 PHASES OF PERSONAL BRANDING

Discover

The first step on your journey toward creating an impactful personal brand is the Discover phase. This isn't just the opening act; it's the foundation upon which everything else is built. You'll delve deep into market research, conduct self-assessments, and analyse competitive landscapes. Expect questions and exercises designed to help you grasp your brand's existing image and space in the market. As you navigate this section, consider yourself a brand archaeologist, unearthing core values, unique selling propositions, and untapped niches. With each revelation, you will gather the essential knowledge that informs your next moves.

Define

Once you've discovered the foundational elements of your brand, it's time to move on to the Define phase. Clarity is the currency here. This is where you'll articulate your vision, identify your target audience, and formulate your mission statement. This section aims to transform all the data and reflective insights into a laser-focused action plan. Whether you are rebranding or starting anew, the exercises in this phase serve as your branding compass, ensuring you stay on track.

Develop

With the groundwork laid and a clear direction set, you'll enter the Develop phase. Imagine this as your brand's drafting table, a place where ideas morph into actionable strategies. From defining your brand voice and personality to laying down a positioning statement, you'll craft a brand identity that aligns seamlessly with your goals and audience needs. And this isn't merely academic—the fun part where you'll blend analytical insights with creative intuition to sculpt a brand persona that genuinely resonates.

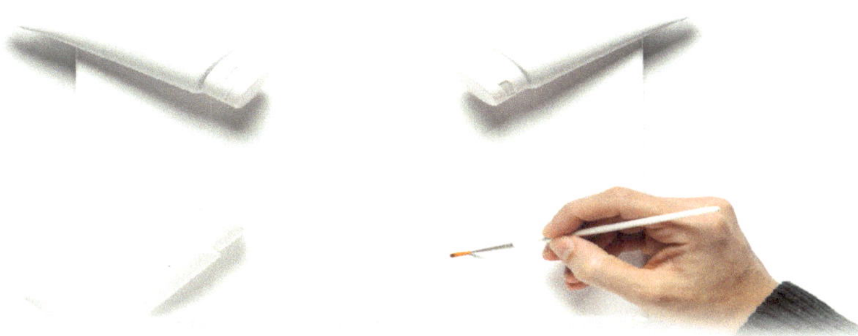

Deliver

In the Deliver phase, your brand leaves the drawing board and enters the real world. This section is action-packed and filled with digital media strategies, content planning, and audience engagement. You've got a brand identity; now it's time to put it to work. This section is like a launchpad; it's designed to propel your brand out of planning mode and into real-world interaction. But remember, successful delivery is not just about the grand launch; it's about sustaining that momentum with consistent and authentic engagement.

Drive

You've discovered, defined, developed, and delivered your brand. So, what's next? Now comes the Drive phase, the engine room where your brand gains steam. This isn't a one-off effort but a continuous cycle of refining, measuring, and enhancing. Branding is a marathon, not a sprint, and this section is your ongoing training regimen. You'll learn techniques for optimising your brand's performance, whether through analytics, SEO, or consumer feedback. Furthermore, you'll explore resilience building and contingency planning, arming your brand for the long haul.

In each phase, you'll find a blend of expert advice, real-world case studies, and practical exercises tailored to lead you through the complex yet exhilarating process of personal branding. By following this structured approach, you'll understand the intricacies of each phase and how they seamlessly flow into each other, contributing to the ultimate goal: turning you into a standout personal brand.

So, are you ready to embark on this comprehensive journey? Turn the page, and let's get started!

The Ultimate Personal Brand Checklist isn't just a list; it's a treasure trove of experiential wisdom and tested methodologies. This book is designed to serve as an evergreen guide to anyone looking to build, refine, or pivot their personal brand. It strategically dissects every facet of branding, from mission statements and online presence to financial planning and crisis management. By the end of this audit, you'll possess not just a snapshot of your current brand health but also a dynamic blueprint for future growth and innovation.

So, are you ready to turn your personal brand ON? Let's dive in.

CHAPTER 3

DISCOVER

In the Discover phase, the focus is on gathering intelligence. This is the groundwork where you dig deep to understand the DNA of your brand, the mindset of your customers, and the competitive landscape you're in. It's essential to capture a 360-degree view of your brand's current state. This information will be the cornerstone for informed decisions down the line.

Brand Research

The "Brand Research" section serves as the foundation for informed decision-making in your personal branding journey. This is where you dig deep to understand yourself and the market landscape you're operating in. Whether it's conducting a competitive analysis to pinpoint your unique market position or utilising SWOT analysis to gauge your brand's Strengths, Weaknesses, Opportunities, and Threats, the focus here is on actionable insights. Beyond that, staying attuned to industry trends and receiving honest feedback is crucial for evolving your brand. Metrics also come into play, with the importance of setting key performance indicators (KPIs) that align with your brand objectives. Ultimately, this section emphasises the need for continuous learning and adaptation through ongoing market research.

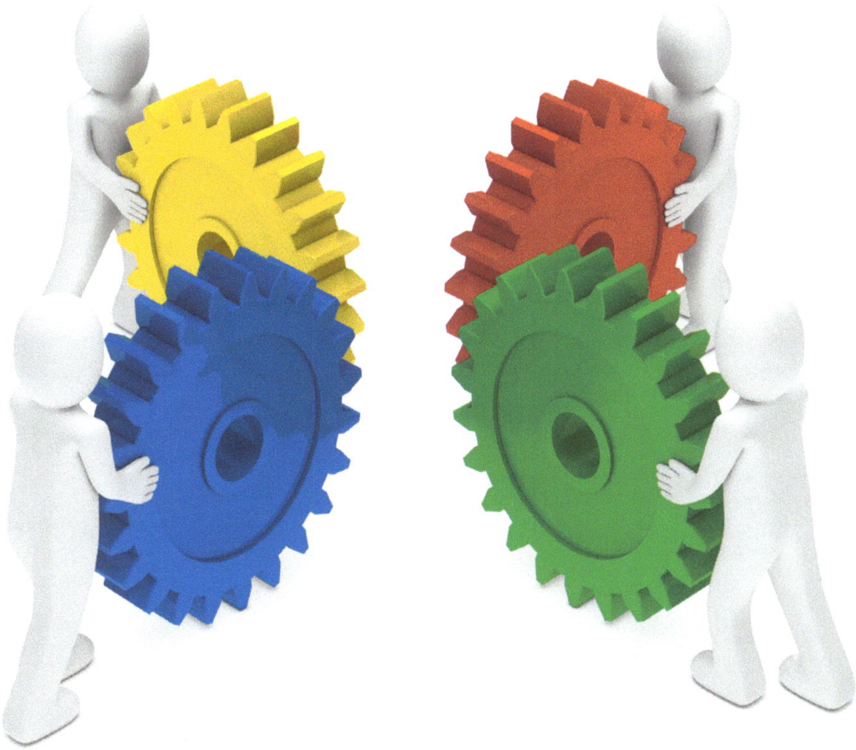

1 Market Positioning

Have you conducted a market and competitor survey/analysis to identify your brand's positioning within the market?

Yes ☐ **No** ☐

2 SWOT Analysis

Do you have a SWOT (Strengths, Weaknesses, Opportunities, Threats) analysis in place?

Yes ☐ **No** ☐

3 Industry Trends

Are you aware of the trends and developments that are emerging in your industry?

Yes ☐ **No** ☐

4 Audience Feedback

Have you solicited and analysed feedback from clients, peers, or mentors about your brand?

Yes ☐ **No** ☐

5 Performance Metrics

Do you regularly measure your personal brand's performance metrics, such as reach, engagement, and conversion?

Yes ☐ **No** ☐

6 KPI Alignment

Have you identified key performance indicators (KPIs) that align with your personal brand goals?

Yes ☐ **No** ☐

7 Adaptive Strategy

Do you have an ongoing strategy for your current target market to adapt and evolve?

Yes ☐ **No** ☐

What I need to do here:

Understanding Your Competition

Understanding Your Competition section is crucial for establishing your unique value in a crowded professional landscape. It's not merely about identifying who else is in your field; it's about gaining a deep understanding of their brand strategy, value proposition, and professional activities. You can better articulate what sets you apart by scrutinising their positioning and pricing models. It's also essential to assess the strengths and weaknesses of others to identify opportunities for your own growth or differentiation. Consistent monitoring of your competitor's social media presence and professional activities can offer invaluable insights into market trends. Keeping an eye on any significant changes, like collaborations or shifts in focus, can also provide an edge. This section prepares you to match the competition and outshine them by playing to your unique strengths.

1 Competitor Identification

Have you identified your top competitors?

Yes ☐ No ☐

2 Positioning Awareness

Do you understand your competitors' brand positioning and value proposition?

Yes ☐ No ☐

3 Pricing Knowledge

Are you aware of your competitors' pricing strategies?

Yes ☐ No ☐

4 SWOT Evaluation

Have you evaluated the strengths and weaknesses of your competitors' product or service offerings?

Yes ☐ No ☐

5 Marketing Oversight

Do you regularly monitor your competitors' marketing and sales channels?

Yes ☐ No ☐

6 Social Media Insight

Have you conducted a social media analysis to gauge your competitors' online presence and engagement?

Yes ☐ No ☐

7 Strategic Updates

Are you updated with recent changes in your competitors' strategy, such as mergers, partnerships, or market expansion?

Yes ☐ No ☐

What I need to do here:

CHAPTER 4

DEFINE

The Define section is all about focus and clarity. Here, you'll hone in on your brand's goals and zero in on the audience you aim to serve. The key is to establish a clear and actionable roadmap. Knowing where you're going and who you're serving can transform a nebulous vision into a tangible strategy.

Goals and Objectives

In personal branding, the "Goals and Objectives" section serves as your roadmap for success. It's not just about ambition; it's about precision and strategic planning. Short-term and long-term goals should align with your brand's mission and vision to maintain coherence in your professional journey. Whether you aim to expand your network, improve skill sets, or achieve particular career milestones, these goals need to be SMART—Specific, Measurable, Achievable, Relevant, and Time-bound. This focus ensures that you're not just dreaming big but also acting decisively, tracking your progress, and adjusting as necessary to stay on the path to achieving your aspirations.

1 Short-term Planning

Have you outlined your short-term goals for the next 6-12 months?

Yes ☐ **No** ☐

2 Long-term Vision

Have you outlined your long-term goals for the next 3-5 years?

Yes ☐ **No** ☐

3 Mission Alignment

Are these goals in alignment with your brand, brand mission and brand vision?

Yes ☐ **No** ☐

4 SMART Goals

Are your goals **S**pecific, **M**easurable, **A**chievable, **R**elevant, and **T**ime-bound?

Yes ☐ **No** ☐

What I need to do here:

Target Audience

Understanding your target audience is indispensable for creating resonant and impactful messaging in personal branding. This section encourages you to dive deep into the characteristics, needs, and preferences of the people you aim to influence or serve. Begin with 'Persona Definition' to sketch detailed profiles of your audience sub-groups. Next, assess their needs with 'Needs Assessment' to tailor your offerings effectively. 'Engagement Strategy' will prompt you to conceptualise creative ways to capture and sustain interest. At the same time, 'Customer Journey' asks you to map out touchpoints, optimising opportunities to influence your audience at various stages of their interaction with your brand.

1 Persona Definition

Have you defined your target audience personas?

Yes ☐ **No** ☐

2 Needs Assessment

Do you understand and address the needs of your audience?

Yes ☐ **No** ☐

3 Engagement Strategy

Do you have strategies for engaging and retaining your audience?

Yes ☐ **No** ☐

4 Customer Journey

Is the customer journey mapped and optimised on how you can impact your customers at different stages of their journey with you?

Yes ☐ **No** ☐

5 Preferred Channels

Have you identified the most effective platforms and mediums to reach your target audience?

Yes ☐ **No** ☐

What I need to do here:

Emotional Connection

The "Emotional Connection" section is crucial for personal brands aiming to build lasting relationships with their audience. This section digs deep into the elements contributing to a strong emotional bond between you and your audience. From gauging customer loyalty to active community building, it emphasises the importance of connecting on an emotional level. Feedback mechanisms are essential for understanding your audience's emotional state and needs. Emotional intelligence allows you to respond to these needs effectively, further strengthening your brand's appeal. Social responsibility adds another layer, demonstrating your brand's commitment to contributing positively to society or a particular cause.

1 Customer Loyalty

Do you have repeat clients or customers?

Yes ☐ **No** ☐

2 Community Building

Are you actively building a community around your brand?

Yes ☐ **No** ☐

3 Feedback Mechanisms

Do you have a system for collecting and analysing emotional feedback?

Yes ☐ **No** ☐

4 Emotional Intelligence

How well do you read and react to your audience's needs?

Yes ☐ **No** ☐

5 Social Responsibility

Does your brand contribute to the community or a cause?

Yes ☐ **No** ☐

What I need to do here:

Personal Branding for Employees

The "Personal Branding for Employees" section is tailored for individuals who want to leverage their personal brand within a corporate setting. This isn't just about how you appear on paper but also how you conduct yourself daily in your work environment. The section starts with defining your identity by identifying the core skills and values you want to embody as an employee. Consistency in demonstrating these traits and receiving feedback from mentors and colleagues ensures your brand is authentic and respected. Through internal discussions and other platforms, visibility within the company helps enhance your brand's reach. Additionally, it's vital to continuously seek out opportunities for skill development and networking that align with your personal brand. The section also includes advice on building resilience, preparing you to tackle setbacks that could otherwise negatively affect your reputation in the workplace.

1 Identity

Have you identified the core skills and values you want to embody in your role as an employee?

Yes ☐ **No** ☐

2 Consistency

How consistently do you display these qualities in your work and interactions with colleagues and superiors?

Yes ☐ **No** ☐

3 Feedback

Do you have mentors or colleagues who can provide honest feedback about your professionalism and contributions?

Yes ☐ **No** ☐

4 Visibility

Are you contributing to internal discussions, workshops, or presentations that can showcase your skills and areas of Expertise?

Yes ☐ **No** ☐

5 Value

How are you leveraging your employee brand to add value to your team and the broader organisation?

Yes ☐ **No** ☐

6 Development

Are you seeking opportunities for skill development and networking that align with your personal brand?

Yes ☐ **No** ☐

7 Resilience

Do you have a plan in place to manage any professional setbacks or challenges that could affect your brand as an employee?

Yes ☐ **No** ☐

What I need to do here:

Personal Branding for C-Suite/Senior Leaders

The "Personal Branding for C-Suite" section is designed for high-level executives aiming to curate and amplify their brand at the pinnacle of corporate leadership. In the C-Suite, your brand doesn't just affect you; it has a ripple effect throughout the entire organisation. This section focuses on strategic brand management that aligns with corporate objectives without losing the individual's unique identity. It covers critical areas like thought leadership, stakeholder management, and brand alignment within the broader organisational culture. The importance of being receptive to feedback and adaptability in the face of rapid corporate and market changes is also emphasised.

1 Thought Leadership

Are you actively contributing to industry conversations, whether through articles, public speaking, or social media?

Yes ☐ **No** ☐

2 Stakeholder Management

How effectively are you leveraging your brand to engage stakeholders like board members, investors, and employees?

Yes ☐ **No** ☐

3 Organisational Alignment

Does your personal brand harmonise with your organisation's broader mission and vision?

Yes ☐ **No** ☐

4 Market Adaptability

How agile is your personal brand in adapting to market changes and shifts in business strategy?

Yes ☐ **No** ☐

5 Impact Measurement

Do you have key performance indicators (KPIs) in place to measure the impact and performance of your personal brand on the organisation?

Yes ☐ **No** ☐

6 Legacy Planning

Have you considered how your personal brand will influence your professional legacy within and outside the organisation?

Yes ☐ **No** ☐

What I need to do here:

Personal Branding at Different Life Stages

Personal branding isn't a one-size-fits-all proposition; it evolves with you as you navigate through different phases of your life. This section illuminates how you can adapt your personal branding approach to align with your current life stage, thereby maximising its relevance and effectiveness.

As a student, your personal brand may focus on showcasing your academic achievements, extracurricular activities, and eagerness to learn and adapt. At this juncture, the potential and promise you offer are your key selling points.

Mid-career professionals need a more nuanced approach. At this stage, your brand should reflect your expertise, accomplishments, and the unique value you bring to your field. Networking and thought leadership, whether through publishing articles or speaking engagements, can be particularly impactful here.

For those nearing retirement, the personal brand might pivot towards legacy. How do you want to be remembered? What wisdom or insights can you share with those following in your footsteps? This could be the time to mentor others, consult, or even write a book.

1 Life Stage Assessment

Where are you currently in your life and career, and how does your personal brand reflect that?

Yes ☐ **No** ☐

2 Adaptability

How often do you reassess your brand attributes to ensure they align with your evolving life stage?

Yes ☐ **No** ☐

3 Skill Highlight

Are the skills and experiences you highlight appropriate for your current life stage?

Yes ☐ **No** ☐

4 Networking Scope

Does your network include contacts who are relevant to your career and life stage?

Yes ☐ **No** ☐

5 Content Relevance

Is the content you produce or share aligned with your current phase and future aspirations?

Yes ☐ **No** ☐

6 Legacy Planning

If you're nearing retirement, what steps are you taking to ensure your personal brand leaves a lasting impression?

Yes ☐ **No** ☐

7 Digital Footprint

Does your online presence accurately reflect your brand as suitable for your life stage?

Yes ☐ **No** ☐

8 Mentorship

Have you sought or provided mentorship to enrich your brand and that of others, particularly if you are at opposite life stages?

Yes ☐ **No** ☐

9 Retrospective Analysis

Have you looked back on your branding journey to analyse insights that could benefit your current stage?

Yes ☐ **No** ☐

What I need to do here:

Social Selling and Personal Branding

In today's digitally connected world, personal branding and social selling go hand in hand. This section focuses on the nexus between your online persona and sales strategy. It outlines how to seamlessly integrate your personal brand into social selling techniques, allowing for a cohesive and authentic customer experience. Leveraging social platforms not only amplifies your brand reach but also enables targeted engagement, building trust and forming long-term relationships with potential buyers. This dynamic approach to sales is about adding value and building connections rather than just closing deals.

1 Content Strategy

What type of content are you sharing on social media to align with your personal brand and attract your target audience?

Yes ☐ **No** ☐

2 Engagement Metrics

How are you measuring engagement and interaction on your social media channels? Are these metrics aligned with your sales goals?

Yes ☐ **No** ☐

3 Network Expansion

Are you strategically expanding your online network to include potential clients, industry experts, and influencers who align with your personal brand?

Yes ☐ **No** ☐

4 Customer Relationships

How are you using social media to deepen relationships with existing customers/stakeholders and encourage repeat business?

Yes ☐ **No** ☐

5 Trust Building

Are you providing valuable and authentic content that establishes you as an industry expert and builds trust among your audience?

Yes ☐ **No** ☐

6 Response Management

How quickly and effectively are you responding to queries, comments, or concerns raised on social media platforms?

Yes ☐ **No** ☐

7 Sales Funnel Integration

How well is your social selling strategy integrated into your overall sales funnel? Are there clear pathways from social engagement to transaction?

Yes ☐ **No** ☐

What I need to do here:

CHAPTER 5

DEVELOP

The Develop phase is where things start getting exciting. Here, you'll craft your brand's strategy by moulding its DNA, pinpointing differentiators, laying out your positioning, and shaping its personality. This isn't just theory; it's the alchemy of turning insights into a dynamic brand identity that resonates with your target audience.

Brand Identity and Mission

Your Brand Identity and Mission serve as the North Star of your personal brand, guiding every action, decision, and strategy you employ. This section aims to ensure that your mission is not just words on a page but serves as a compelling call to action. From crafting a resonant mission statement to defining your core values, the objective here is to have a deep-rooted foundation that resonates with both you and your target audience. Answering these questions will help you align your actions with your aspirations, creating a consistent and impactful brand experience.

1 Brand Mission Statement

Is it clear, concise, and inspiring?

Yes ☐ **No** ☐

2 Vision Statement

Does it align with your long-term goals?

Yes ☐ **No** ☐

3 Value Proposition

What sets you apart from competitors?

Yes ☐ No ☐

4 Core Values

Are they defined and communicated?

Yes ☐ No ☐

What I need to do here:

Differentiation and Positioning

In a marketplace saturated with look-alikes and sound-alikes, differentiation and positioning are paramount to establishing a memorable and influential personal brand. This section focuses on the facets that set you apart from the crowd and how you strategically position those unique attributes in the minds of your target audience. From identifying your Unique Selling Proposition (USP) to ensuring that your visual identity and messaging align with that positioning, these questions serve as a roadmap for carving out a distinct niche. By the end of this section, you should have a clear idea of your brand's unique attributes and how best to leverage them for competitive advantage.

1 USP Identification

Have you identified your unique selling proposition (USP)?

Yes ☐ No ☐

2 Brand Attributes

Does your brand have specific attributes that set it apart from competitors?

Yes ☐ No ☐

3 Emotional Benefits

Have you considered your brand's emotional benefits to consumers?

Yes ☐ No ☐

4 Positioning Statement

Do you have a clear brand positioning statement?

Yes ☐ **No** ☐

5 Market Research

Have you tested your brand's positioning with a focus group or other forms of market research?

Yes ☐ **No** ☐

6 Visual Alignment

Is your brand's visual identity aligned with its positioning?

Yes ☐ **No** ☐

7 Feature Superiority

Are your product or service features distinctly different or superior to your competitors?

Yes ☐ **No** ☐

8 Voice Consistency

Does your brand voice and messaging consistently reinforce your positioning?

Yes ☐ **No** ☐

9 Positioning Matrix

Have you mapped out a positioning matrix to visually understand where you stand compared to competitors?

Yes ☐ **No** ☐

10 Marketing Alignment

Is your marketing strategy aligned to promote your brand's unique position in the market?

Yes ☐ **No** ☐

What I need to do here:

Brand Personality

Navigating the realm of personal branding isn't just about what you offer—it's also about how you present it. Your brand personality acts as the emotional and psychological relationship your brand establishes with your audience, serving as a critical component of how they experience and interact with your offerings. This section aims to help you clearly define and consistently convey your brand personality across various touchpoints. Questions range from the basics of identifying core traits and aligning them with business objectives to more nuanced considerations like audience appeal and team training. Ultimately, this section guides you in creating a compelling, consistent, and resonant personality for your brand.

1 Core Traits

Have you defined the core traits that make up your brand personality?

Yes ☐ **No** ☐

2 Business Alignment

Does your brand personality align with your overall business objectives?

Yes ☐ **No** ☐

3 Communication Style

Have you identified the tone and style of communication that mirrors your brand personality?

Yes ☐ **No** ☐

4 Touchpoint Consistency

Is your brand personality consistently reflected across all touchpoints, both online and offline?

Yes ☐ **No** ☐

5 Audience Appeal

Have you considered how your brand personality will appeal to your target audience?

Yes ☐ **No** ☐

6 Audience Appeal

Does your brand's visual identity (colour, typography, imagery) resonate with its personality?

Yes ☐ **No** ☐

7 Team Training

Is your team trained to embody the brand personality in customer interactions?

Yes ☐ **No** ☐

8 Content Guidelines

Do you have guidelines to ensure that content creators adhere to your brand personality?

Yes ☐ **No** ☐

9 Consumer Perception

Have you evaluated consumer perception to confirm that your intended personality is what's actually being communicated?

Yes ☐ **No** ☐

10 Relevance Check

Are you regularly updating and revisiting your brand personality to ensure it stays relevant and effective?

Yes ☐ **No** ☐

What I need to do here:

Brand Story

Your brand's story is more than a narrative; it's the cohesive thread that connects you with your audience on an emotional level. It provides context, builds credibility, and enhances relatability. This section walks you through the process of crafting a compelling brand story that aligns with your mission and vision. From identifying your brand's origins and key milestones to ensuring its emotional resonance with your target audience, these questions are designed to make your brand story a living entity. It's not just about what's been written or said; it's about ongoing storytelling that evolves and integrates across all your customer touchpoints. This dynamic approach keeps your brand story relevant, engaging, and authentic.

1 Story Elements

Have you identified the key elements that make up your brand's origin story?

Yes ☐ **No** ☐

2 Mission Alignment

Does your brand story align with your company mission and vision?

Yes ☐ **No** ☐

3 Relatability Factors

Have you articulated the challenges, triumphs, and milestones that make your brand relatable?

Yes ☐ **No** ☐

4 Story Clarity

Is your brand story simple, memorable, and easy to understand?

Yes ☐ No ☐

5 Solving a Problem

Is there a specific problem that your brand was founded to solve?

Yes ☐ No ☐

6 Value Integration

Does your story include the values that guide your brand's decisions and actions?

Yes ☐ No ☐

7 Emotional Engagement

Have you considered how your brand story will emotionally engage your target audience?

Yes ☐ No ☐

8 Channel Consistency

Is your brand story consistently told across all marketing channels?

Yes ☐ No ☐

9 Storytelling Touchpoints

Have you incorporated storytelling elements into your customer touchpoints (website, social media, customer service, etc.)?

Yes ☐ No ☐

10 Story Evolution

Do you regularly update your brand story to reflect your development, milestones and success?

Yes ☐ No ☐

What I need to do here:

Messaging

In a saturated market, not just what you say but how you say it can set you apart. The Messaging section ensures that your brand communicates clearly, consistently, and compellingly. Whether it's the tone you adopt or the succinctness of your elevator pitch, every piece of communication message counts. Here, we also consider the power of customer testimonials and reviews to boost your brand's credibility.

1 Tone and Voice

Is your writing style consistent?

Yes ☐ **No** ☐

2 Elevator Pitch

Can you succinctly articulate your brand?

Yes ☐ **No** ☐

3 Tagline

Do you have a memorable, compelling tagline?

Yes ☐ **No** ☐

4 Testimonials and Reviews

Are they showcased and positive?

Yes ☐ **No** ☐

What I need to do here:

Taglines

A tagline in the context of personal branding serves as a succinct and memorable statement that encapsulates the essence of who you are and what you bring to the table. Just as iconic brands use taglines to become etched in the public consciousness, your personal brand tagline can work as an effective shorthand to convey your value proposition, purpose, or unique selling points. A well-crafted tagline is not just catchy; it also aligns perfectly with your broader brand narrative, thereby adding a layer of coherence and consistency to your brand identity. This section will guide you through the process of formulating or refining a tagline that speaks volumes in just a few words.

1 Alignment

Does your tagline align seamlessly with your personal brand's core message and values?

Yes ☐ **No** ☐

2 Memorability

Is your tagline easy to remember? Does it stick in people's minds after a brief encounter?

Yes ☐ **No** ☐

3 Differentiation

Does the tagline set you apart from competitors or peers in your industry?

Yes ☐ **No** ☐

4 Relevance

Is your tagline applicable to the target audience you aim to serve?

Yes ☐ **No** ☐

5 Simplicity

Is your tagline free from jargon and easily understandable by anyone, regardless of their familiarity with your field?

Yes ☐ **No** ☐

6 Versatility

Can your tagline be used effectively across various platforms and mediums, including social media, business cards, and presentations?

Yes ☐ **No** ☐

7 Authenticity

Does the tagline resonate with your own sense of self? Does it feel true to who you are?

Yes ☐ **No** ☐

8 Impact

Does your tagline evoke the desired emotional or intellectual response from your audience?

Yes ☐ **No** ☐

9 Longevity

Is your tagline timeless, or will it need to be updated to remain relevant in a changing market?

Yes ☐ **No** ☐

What I need to do here:

Elevator Pitch

An elevator pitch is more than just a quick introduction; it's a powerful brand statement condensed into a bite-sized message designed to make an immediate impact. This section hones in on the critical elements that make your elevator pitch compelling and effective. From articulating your core value proposition to ensuring your message connects with your target audience, the objective is to leave an unforgettable impression. Additionally, the pitch should be adaptable in duration, enabling you to engage people in various settings and conclude with a solid call to action that invites further exploration or dialogue with your brand.

1 Core Value Proposition

Does your elevator pitch succinctly explain what sets you apart?

Yes ☐ **No** ☐

2 Target Audience Appeal

Is your pitch designed to catch the attention of your target demographic?

Yes ☐ **No** ☐

3 Duration

Is your pitch concise enough to be delivered in less than a minute and longer if needed?

Yes ☐ **No** ☐

4 Call-to-Action

Does your pitch encourage the listener to engage further with your brand?

Yes ☐ **No** ☐

What I need to do here:

Branded Executive Presence

In the high-stakes world of business, your personal brand isn't just about what you say or do but also how you present yourself. Executive presence is the elusive quality that combines elements like gravitas, confidence, and a polished appearance to create a compelling, authoritative persona. Your clothing, your demeanour, your eloquence—all these are crucial components that help establish your executive presence. In essence, it's about packaging yourself in a manner that is congruent with your brand values and resonates with your target audience segment. This section provides you with insights and questions to evaluate and elevate your executive presence as an integral part of your personal brand.

1 Appearance

Are your clothing choices aligned with the brand image you wish to project?

Yes ☐ No ☐

2 Gravitas

How effectively do you exude confidence and authority in business settings?

Yes ☐ No ☐

3 Communication Skills

Are you articulate and persuasive in your verbal and non-verbal communication?

Yes ☐ No ☐

4 Emotional Intelligence

How well do you read the room and adjust your behaviour to influence others positively?

Yes ☐ No ☐

5 Adaptability

Can you modify your executive presence to suit different audience segments without diluting your brand's essence?

Yes ☐ No ☐

6 Consistency

Is your executive presence consistent across various platforms and interactions, both online and offline?

Yes ☐ No ☐

7 Impression Management

Are you aware of the unconscious biases that might affect how your executive presence is perceived, and do you know how to manage them?

Yes ☐ No ☐

8 Networking

How does your executive presence facilitate or hamper your networking effectiveness?

Yes ☐ No ☐

9 Mentorship

Do you have role models or mentors who exude the type of executive presence you aspire to? What can you learn from them?

Yes ☐ **No** ☐

What I need to do here:

Social Proof Points: Testimonials

Social proof serves as an indispensable pillar in shaping your brand's credibility and trustworthiness. Explicitly focusing on testimonials, this section urges you to consider various forms of endorsements that substantiate your brand's claims and values. From client testimonials that bring your capabilities to life to peer endorsements that give you industry clout and case studies that offer a narrative of your brand's impact, each element is a powerful testament to your skills and expertise. By effectively leveraging these testimonials, you not only validate your brand but also instil confidence in prospective clients and partners.

1 Client Testimonials

Are they showcased on your website and social media platforms?

Yes ☐ **No** ☐

2 Peer Endorsements

Do experts or influencers in your field vouch for you?

Yes ☐ **No** ☐

3 Case Studies

Do you have detailed stories showcasing your Expertise and the value you've provided to clients?

Yes ☐ **No** ☐

What I need to do here:

Social Proof Points: Media Features/Awards

In the realm of brand credibility, media features and awards serve as invaluable social proof that your brand is recognised and esteemed. This section invites you to explore and showcase your media mentions, from reputable news sources to industry journals, as they serve as third-party validations of your competence and innovation. Equally important are awards and recognitions, which not only celebrate your accomplishments but also position you as an authority in your field. Featuring these achievements prominently in your branding strategy helps build trust and credibility among your audience.

1 Press Mentions

Have you been mentioned or featured in credible publications?

Yes ☐ No ☐

2 Awards and Recognitions

Are any awards you've won visible, and do they align with your brand?

Yes ☐ No ☐

What I need to do here:

Social Proof Points: Credibility

Credibility is the bedrock of any successful personal brand. This section delves into the various elements that can enhance your brand's trustworthiness and authority. From relevant certifications and degrees to publications that highlight your expertise, each of these aspects contributes to a compelling narrative of competence and reliability. A transparent track record and measurable success metrics further solidify your credibility, giving your audience concrete reasons to trust and engage with you. Consider also showcasing success stories or case studies, as these real-world examples serve as compelling testimonials to your skills and effectiveness.

1 Certifications and Degrees

Are they showcased and aligned with your brand?

Yes ☐ No ☐

2 Publications

Have you published articles, books, or papers that establish you as an expert?

Yes ☐ No ☐

3 Track Record

Is your career experience transparent and easily accessible?

Yes ☐ No ☐

4 Success Metrics

Are you displaying quantifiable metrics of your past work to showcase your skills?

Yes ☐ **No** ☐

5 Showcasing

Do you showcase your success stories or case studies?

Yes ☐ **No** ☐

What I need to do here:

Social Proof Points: Thought Leadership

Thought leadership is a critical dimension of brand authority, allowing you to rise above the noise and command attention in your field. This section explores key activities that can position you as a thought leader. Creating expert content, whether it's articles, research papers, or blog posts, demonstrates your depth of knowledge and contributes to industry discussions. Authoring a book can elevate your brand to a new level of respect and recognition. Moreover, engaging in public speaking opportunities such as webinars, podcasts, or live events allows you to directly influence and inspire your audience, further solidifying your reputation as a leader in your domain.

1 Expert Content

Are you producing content that sets you apart as a thought leader in your industry?

Yes ☐ **No** ☐

2 Book

Have you written a book which showcases your Expertise in the topic that showcases your thought leadership?

Yes ☐ **No** ☐

3 Public Speaking

Are you influencing people through webinars, podcasts, or speaking engagements?

Yes ☐ **No** ☐

What I need to do here:

Social Proof Points: Network Influence

In today's interconnected world, who you know often matters as much as what you know. This section dives into the aspects of your brand that demonstrate your networking prowess and influence. Being associated with high-profile individuals within your industry can validate your credibility, serving as a strong endorsement of your expertise. Active participation in industry groups, forums, and social media communities not only amplifies your reach but also positions you as a go-to expert whose opinions are valued. Collaborations with influencers in content creation further expand your audience and bolster your reputation, providing another layer of social proof to your brand.

1 High-Profile Connections

Are you associated with influential people within or related to your industry?

Yes ☐ **No** ☐

2 Community Influence

Are you part of industry groups, forums, or social media communities where your opinions are valued?

Yes ☐ **No** ☐

3 Collaboration

Have you partnered with influencers to produce content?

Yes ☐ **No** ☐

What I need to do here:

CHAPTER 6

DELIVER

Now comes the moment of truth: the Deliver phase. This is where your brand comes alive and interacts with the world. Leveraging a robust set of brand assets and strategic digital media approaches, you'll deploy your brand through focused content marketing efforts. It's not just about launching; it's about landing—right into the hearts and minds of your audience.

Visual Branding

Visual branding isn't just aesthetic; it's an integral part of your brand identity that communicates your values, personality, and promise at a glance. This section delves into the essentials of creating a cohesive and impactful visual brand. From the logo that symbolises your ethos to the consistent use of colour schemes and typography that align with your brand persona, every element is scrutinised. Additionally, business cards and other branded materials should be a seamless extension of this visual language. High-quality imagery and specialised language further fine-tune your brand's visual narrative, creating a memorable and authentic impression.

1 Logo

Does it resonate with your brand values?

Yes ☐ **No** ☐

2 Colour Scheme

Are your brand colours consistently used?

Yes ☐ **No** ☐

3 Typography

Is your chosen font aligned with your brand persona?

Yes ☐ **No** ☐

4 Business Card

Does it reflect your brand identity?

Yes ☐ **No** ☐

5 Photography/Imagery

Are your images high-quality and consistent?

Yes ☐ **No** ☐

6 Language

Have you created brand-led words, phrases or communication?

Yes ☐ No ☐

What I need to do here:

The Psychology of Colour

The role of colour in personal branding is often underestimated, but it's a powerful psychological tool that can significantly impact how you are perceived. This section delves into the science and psychology behind colour choices in various brand assets—such as logos, websites, and attire—and how these choices affect public perception. Colour isn't just a design element; it communicates mood, evokes emotion, and even influences behaviour. Hence, understanding the psychology of colour can elevate your brand from not just being seen but also truly understood.

Various colours elicit different psychological reactions. For example, blue often conveys trust and reliability, making it a frequent choice for corporate brands. Red, on the other hand, is eye-catching and can evoke feelings of passion or urgency. Earth tones like green and brown can communicate a sense of balance or environmental consciousness. On a personal level, the colours you wear can also speak volumes. For instance, black might signify sophistication or luxury, while bright colours could indicate creativity and innovation.

1 Logo Colour

Have you chosen a colour for your logo that aligns with the message you want to convey?

Yes ☐ No ☐

2 Website Palette

Does the colour scheme of your website engage your audience and reflect the emotions you aim to elicit?

Yes ☐ No ☐

3 Attire Choices

Are you consciously selecting clothing colours for public appearances that complement your personal brand attributes?

Yes ☐ No ☐

4 Content Colours

Are the colours used in your branded content consistent and in alignment with your brand's message?

Yes ☐ No ☐

5 Emotional Impact

Have you researched how different colours affect emotions and, subsequently, the perception of your brand?

Yes ☐ No ☐

6 Cultural Considerations

Are you aware of how colour meanings can vary between different cultures, and have you accounted for this in your branding if you operate in a multicultural environment?

Yes ☐ No ☐

7 Accessibility

Have you considered colour accessibility, such as colour contrast for readability on digital platforms, to ensure your brand is inclusive?

Yes ☐ No ☐

8 Psychological Alignment

Does your colour scheme align with the psychological traits you wish to emphasise (e.g., red for excitement, blue for trust, green for growth)?

Yes ☐ No ☐

9 Testing and Feedback

Have you tested multiple colour schemes and gathered feedback to assess how they resonate with your target audience?

Yes ☐ No ☐

What I need to do here:

Brand Assets

In today's multifaceted personal branding landscape, your brand assets serve as your toolkit for engagement and impact. These tangible and intangible assets encompass a wide array of elements, from traditional aspects like your logo and written content to modern facets like video and audio resources. Each asset plays a specific role in building your brand's identity and amplifying its message. Much like how businesses manage their assets for maximum return on investment, your brand assets demand the same level of strategic care and attention. This section is designed to guide you through an audit of your existing assets, evaluate their effectiveness, and pinpoint opportunities for development and enhancement.

1 Logo and Visual Identity

Does your logo and overall visual scheme consistently encapsulate your brand's ethos?

Yes ☐ No ☐

2 Website and Blog

Is your website up-to-date, user-friendly, and reflective of your personal brand?

Yes ☐ No ☐

3 Content Library

Do you have a library of high-quality articles, videos, and podcasts that provide valuable insights to your audience?

Yes ☐ No ☐

4 Audio Resources

Are you utilising audio mediums like podcasts or audiobooks to extend your brand's reach?

Yes ☐ No ☐

5 Video Portfolio

Do you have a curated set of professional videos that effectively communicate your brand message?

Yes ☐ **No** ☐

6 Templates

Do you have branded templates for presentations, invoices, or other business-related documents?

Yes ☐ **No** ☐

7 Social Media Presence

Are your social media profiles/channels well integrated to represent your personal brand narrative to your audience?

Yes ☐ **No** ☐

8 Email List

Are you actively cultivating and engaging with your email list, a crucial direct-to-audience asset?

Yes ☐ **No** ☐

9 Testimonials and Reviews

Have you accrued and displayed authentic testimonials that support your credibility and expertise?

Yes ☐ **No** ☐

10 Offline Assets

Do you possess physical marketing materials, such as business cards or brochures, that are congruent with your online brand?

Yes ☐ **No** ☐

11 Intellectual Property

Are you creating or do you own proprietary content, processes, or patented elements that differentiate you?

Yes ☐ **No** ☐

What I need to do here:

Online Presence

In today's digitally connected world, your online presence serves as the global storefront for your personal brand. From your personal website as a central hub to your LinkedIn profile that showcases your professional expertise, each digital touchpoint needs to reflect a cohesive brand image and message. What Google says about you is equally important—proactively managing your search results and online reputation is critical. Implementing SEO strategies can boost your content's visibility, while analytics offer actionable insights to refine your approach. Don't underestimate the power of a well-curated blog, engaging multimedia content, and a compelling e-newsletter to position you as a thought leader and keep your audience engaged.

1 Personal Website

Is it up-to-date and reflective of your brand?

Yes ☐ No ☐

2 LinkedIn Profile

Does it showcase your skills, Expertise, and personality?

Yes ☐ No ☐

3 Social Media

Are your profiles consistent in image and messaging?

Yes ☐ No ☐

4 Google Search

What comes up when you Google your name?

Yes ☐ No ☐

5 Content

Is your published content aligned with your brand?

Yes ☐ No ☐

6 SEO Optimisation

Are you employing SEO best practices to ensure your content reaches your target audience?

Yes ☐ No ☐

7 Blog

Do you maintain a blog that positions you as a thought leader in your field?

Yes ☐ No ☐

8 Analytics

Are you tracking and analysing metrics to gauge the effectiveness of your online presence?

Yes ☐ No ☐

9 Reputation Management

Do you regularly monitor and address reviews, comments, and other forms of feedback online?

Yes ☐ No ☐

10 Multimedia

Are you utilising videos, podcasts, or webinars to diversify the types of content you offer?

Yes ☐ **No** ☐

11 E-Newsletter

Do you engage your audience through periodic e-newsletters that offer value?

Yes ☐ **No** ☐

What I need to do here:

Content Strategy

In the intricate landscape of personal branding, your content strategy acts as the conductor of your brand's symphony. This isn't merely a collection of random tactics; it's a well-composed, long-term strategy harmonising different elements. A meticulously curated content calendar is your score, guiding the pacing and timing of your brand's messaging to match the ever-evolving needs and curiosities of your target audience. Your content mix—encompassing blogs, podcasts, videos, whitepapers, and infographics—represents the various instruments in your ensemble, each adding unique tones and textures to your brand narrative. But remember, having multiple tools is not enough; they must be finely tuned (relevant) and played by expert hands (quality) to create a captivating symphony. Consistent and regular posting serves as the rhythm, keeping your audience engaged and underlining your brand's credibility and reach.

1 Content Calendar

Do you have a structured calendar that outlines when and what to post?

Yes ☐ **No** ☐

6 Content Diversity

Are you leveraging a mix of blogs, podcasts, videos, whitepapers, and infographics for a richer brand story?

Yes ☐ **No** ☐

3 Messaging Formats

Are you using storytelling, how-to guides, or listicles to make the content more engaging?

Yes ☐ No ☐

4 Content Relevance

Does your content directly address the questions, challenges, or interests of your target audience?

Yes ☐ No ☐

5 Content Quality

Is your content backed by thorough research, well-crafted, and proofread for errors?

Yes ☐ No ☐

6 Content Frequency

Are you maintaining a regular posting schedule that keeps your audience consistently engaged?

Yes ☐ No ☐

7 Creative Flair

Are you infusing your unique personality and creativity into the content to make it truly one-of-a-kind?

Yes ☐ No ☐

8 Multi-platform Consistency

Is your messaging consistent across various platforms, maintaining the integrity of your brand voice?

Yes ☐ No ☐

9 Feedback Loop

Are you using metrics and audience feedback to refine your content strategy continually?

Yes ☐ No ☐

10 Content Lifespan

Are you considering the longevity of your content? Is it evergreen, or does it have a short shelf-life?

Yes ☐ No ☐

What I need to do here:

Social Media

In the ever-evolving digital landscape, mastering your social media presence is crucial for brand success. Whether it's choosing the right platforms or maintaining brand consistency, each aspect requires a strategic approach. Beyond mere posting, engagement is key to building relationships with your audience. KPIs and analytics are your guides to understanding what resonates, helping you tweak strategies in real-time. Having a crisis management plan ensures you're prepared for the unpredictable, while collaborations can widen your reach. Utilising audience insights can help in customising content, and the right hashtag and sponsored content strategies can significantly boost your visibility.

1 Platform Diversity

Are you present on the platforms where your audience spends time?

Yes ☐ No ☐

2 Content Consistency

Is your social media content aligned with your overall brand strategy?

Yes ☐ No ☐

3 Engagement Rate

Are you not just posting but also engaging with your audience?

Yes ☐ No ☐

4 Analytics and KPIs

Are you tracking key performance indicators to measure the success of your social media strategy?

Yes ☐ No ☐

5 Crisis Management

Do you have a plan for handling negative comments or controversies that may arise on social media?

Yes ☐ No ☐

6 Collaborations and Partnerships

Have you partnered with influencers or other brands for social campaigns?

Yes ☐ No ☐

7 Audience Insights

Are you using analytics to gain a deeper understanding of your audience's behaviour and preferences?

Yes ☐ No ☐

8 Hashtag Strategy

Are you using relevant hashtags to increase the visibility of your posts?

Yes ☐ No ☐

9 Sponsored Content

Have you explored paid promotions & advertisements to boost your reach?

Yes ☐ No ☐

What I need to do here:

Community Creation & Engagement

Community creation and engagement aren't just buzzwords; they are critical pillars of modern brand-building. Starting with community building, your focus should be on nurturing a vibrant online ecosystem that reflects your brand's core values and objectives. A growing social following is good, but it needs to translate into active engagement—likes, shares, comments, and especially user-generated content that serves as a peer-to-peer endorsement. Effective community moderation is key to maintaining a positive and constructive environment. Don't overlook the value offering; exclusive content, perks, or rewards can incentivise participation and sustain interest. Feedback mechanisms help you pivot and adapt, while educational content enriches the community. Exploring niche communities and hosting events can deepen engagement and keep your audience coming back for more.

1 Community Building

Are you nurturing an online community around your brand?

Yes ☐ **No** ☐

2 Social Following

Does your follower count reflect your brand's popularity or influence?

Yes ☐ **No** ☐

3 User-Generated Content

Is your audience creating content that showcases your product or service?

Yes ☐ **No** ☐

4 Engagement Metrics

Are you tracking likes, shares, comments, and other interactions to measure community involvement?

Yes ☐ **No** ☐

5 Community Moderation

Do you have guidelines and moderators to manage the community space and handle disputes?

Yes ☐ **No** ☐

6 Value Offering

Are you providing exclusive content, perks, or rewards to community members?

Yes ☐ **No** ☐

7 Community Feedback

Do you have a system for collecting and acting upon feedback from your community?

Yes ☐ **No** ☐

8 Educational Content

Are you offering useful information, webinars, or tutorials that benefit your community?

Yes ☐ **No** ☐

9 Niche Communities

Have you considered creating smaller, more focused communities around specific products or interests related to your brand?

Yes ☐ **No** ☐

10 Event Hosting

Do you hold live Q&A sessions, webinars, or other events to bring the community together?

Yes ☐ **No** ☐

What I need to do here:

Video Marketing

In today's fast-paced digital landscape, video marketing stands as a cornerstone for effective personal branding. It offers the potency of visual storytelling, allowing you to convey complex messages in an accessible format while showcasing your unique brand attributes. The multi-dimensionality of video—encompassing sound, vision, and emotion—creates a compelling medium that fosters more profound connections with your audience. This section aims to demystify the process of incorporating video into your personal brand strategy, emphasising key considerations ranging from types of videos to storytelling elements and essential tools.

1 Content Strategy

What types of video content—webinars, vlogs, tutorials, testimonials—will serve your brand's goals and resonate with your target audience?

Yes ☐ **No** ☐

2 Quality Assurance

Are you maintaining high production values that align with your brand's reputation?

Yes ☐ **No** ☐

3 Platform Suitability

Have you optimised video content for specific platforms like YouTube, LinkedIn, or Instagram?

Yes ☐ **No** ☐

4 Message Consistency

Do your videos harmonise with your brand messaging, goals, and objectives?

Yes ☐ **No** ☐

5 Engagement Metrics

Are you tracking KPIs such as viewer duration, likes, shares, and comments to measure effectiveness?

Yes ☐ **No** ☐

6 SEO Optimisation

Have you used well-researched keywords in your video titles, descriptions, and tags?

Yes ☐ **No** ☐

7 Call to Action

Does each video incorporate a clear CTA to guide viewers on the next steps?

Yes ☐ **No** ☐

8 Accessibility

Are you making your videos universally accessible, offering captions or translations where necessary?

Yes ☐ **No** ☐

9 Frequency & Timing

What is your video publishing schedule, and how does it align with your audience's online activity?

Yes ☐ No ☐

10 Budget & Resources

Have you allocated sufficient resources for consistent, high-quality video production?

Yes ☐ No ☐

11 Story Characters

Are you introducing relatable characters or personas in your video narrative to establish an emotional connection?

Yes ☐ No ☐

12 Tools

Which software and hardware tools—like Adobe Premiere Pro, Final Cut Pro, or simple mobile editing apps—are you utilising for video creation and editing?

Yes ☐ No ☐

13 Interactive Elements

Are you leveraging interactive video features like clickable links, embedded forms, or real-time polls to engage your audience?

Yes ☐ No ☐

What I need to do here:

LinkedIn Mastery

LinkedIn serves as a critical platform for personal branding, especially for professionals aiming to establish credibility, build a network, and create opportunities in the business world. Being active and strategic on this platform can set you apart as an industry leader, job candidate, or business partner. This section will help you review your LinkedIn activities and strategies to ensure you effectively utilise this channel for personal branding.

1 Profile Completeness

Is your LinkedIn profile fully filled out, including a professional photo, compelling headline, and detailed work experience?

Yes ☐ **No** ☐

2 Content Strategy

Are you regularly posting or sharing relevant, high-quality content that resonates with your target audience?

Yes ☐ **No** ☐

3 Engagement

Do you actively engage with your network by commenting, liking, or sharing posts that align with your personal brand?

Yes ☐ **No** ☐

4 Thought Leadership

Are you publishing articles or posts that establish you as an expert in your field?

Yes ☐ **No** ☐

5 Skills & Endorsements

Have you listed the skills that are crucial to your professional persona, and have these skills been endorsed?

Yes ☐ No ☐

6 Recommendations

Have you requested recommendations from colleagues, supervisors, or clients to validate your Expertise and Experience?

Yes ☐ No ☐

7 Personal Branding Story

Does your 'About' section narrate a coherent and compelling story of who you are professionally?

Yes ☐ No ☐

8 Networking

Are you using LinkedIn to grow your network, actively connecting with professionals in your industry or area of interest?

Yes ☐ No ☐

9 Company Affiliation

If applicable, have you linked your profile to your organisation's LinkedIn page, and are you sharing or commenting on its updates?

Yes ☐ No ☐

10 Group Participation

Are you part of LinkedIn Groups that are relevant to your industry, and do you actively participate in them?

Yes ☐ No ☐

11 Job Seeking Visibility

If you're open to new opportunities, have you utilised the platform's features to make this visible to recruiters?

Yes ☐ No ☐

12 LinkedIn Analytics

Do you regularly review analytics to understand the reach and engagement of your posts and articles?

Yes ☐ No ☐

What I need to do here:

Lead Generation

In the context of personal branding, lead generation isn't just about driving business; it's about building meaningful connections that can lead to various types of opportunities—whether that's a job offer, a business partnership, or a consulting gig. The aim is to turn the interest you generate through your personal brand into substantive, actionable relationships. At the crux of this is your ability to showcase your value proposition convincingly and extend your reach through targeted strategies. This section of the audit zeroes in on your lead generation effectiveness, evaluating both the strategies you currently employ and the quality of the leads you're attracting.

1 Target Audience

Have you clearly identified the audience for which your personal brand holds the most relevance and value?

Yes ☐ **No** ☐

2 Value Proposition

Is your unique value proposition well-articulated, compelling, and clearly displayed across your brand touchpoints?

Yes ☐ No ☐

3 Lead Magnets

Do you offer high-value content or services (e.g., eBooks, webinars, free consultations) that entice people to engage with you?

Yes ☐ No ☐

4 SEO & Content Strategy

Are you employing search engine optimisation and creating content that aligns with the interests and needs of your target audience?

Yes ☐ No ☐

5 Social Media Outreach

How effective are your social media platforms in generating interest and interaction from potential leads?

Yes ☐ No ☐

6 Networking

Do you actively engage in both online and offline networking events to meet potential leads?

Yes ☐ No ☐

7 Email Marketing

Are you utilising email campaigns to nurture leads, provide value, and ultimately convert interest into action?

Yes ☐ No ☐

8 Quality Over Quantity

Are you more focused on the number of leads or the quality and relevance of the people you connect with?

Yes ☐ No ☐

9 Follow-up Strategy

Do you have a systematic process for following up with leads to keep them engaged and move them down the sales or engagement funnel?

Yes ☐ No ☐

10 Analytics and Metrics

Are you tracking KPIs related to lead generation and engagement to refine your strategies continually?

Yes ☐ No ☐

11 CRM System

Do you have a Customer Relationship Management (CRM) system in place to organise and manage leads effectively?

Yes ☐ No ☐

12 Referral Program

Have you considered or implemented a referral program to encourage your existing network to introduce you to new opportunities?

Yes ☐ No ☐

What I need to do here:

Career Brand Visibility

While establishing a personal brand typically involves outward-facing activities like social media engagement, thought leadership, and public speaking, it's equally crucial to consider internal activities that elevate your brand within your current workplace. These 'behind-the-scenes' actions can significantly enhance your career visibility, foster stronger relationships, and set you apart as an invaluable asset to your organisation.

1 Going the Extra Mile

Are you known among colleagues for always going above and beyond in your contributions? Are you proactive in identifying problems and offering solutions?

Yes ☐ No ☐

2 Volunteering for Internal Events

Do you take an active role in internal staff events, not just as a participant but as an organiser or contributor?

Yes ☐ No ☐

3 Contributing to In-House Articles

Are you lending your expertise and voice to in-house publications, newsletters, or the company blog?

Yes ☐ No ☐

4 Stepping Up as a Brand Ambassador

Do you take pride in representing your organisation at external events, on social media, or in your wider professional network?

Yes ☐ No ☐

5 Finding a Mentor with Seniority

Have you sought mentorship from a more senior colleague or leader within the organisation to aid your career development?

Yes ☐ No ☐

6 Contributing to Team Members' Growth

Do you offer help or guidance to colleagues, effectively contributing to a positive work culture and their professional growth?

Yes ☐ No ☐

7 Sharing the Organisational Brand

Are you an advocate for your company's brand values, sharing accomplishments and initiatives externally through your channels?

Yes ☐ No ☐

8 Demonstrating Brand Values to Leadership

Do you make it a point to align your contributions and behaviour with the company's brand values, and do your superiors recognise this alignment?

Yes ☐ No ☐

9 Professional Development

Are you taking advantage of any training or learning opportunities provided by your workplace to continually improve and add value to the team?

Yes ☐ **No** ☐

10 Alignment with Corporate Objectives

Does your personal branding strategy align with your company's goals, and are you clear on how your brand adds value to the organisation?

Yes ☐ **No** ☐

11 Internal Network Building

Are you expanding your internal network, not only horizontally among peers but also vertically, to gain a more well-rounded view of your organisation?

Yes ☐ **No** ☐

What I need to do here:

Pitching Your Personal Brand

The ability to articulate your personal brand quickly and compellingly is an invaluable asset, whether you are networking, interviewing for a job, or seeking new business opportunities. A well-crafted pitch can serve as the linchpin that connects all the elements of your brand and concisely communicates its essence. This section is designed to guide you through refining your personal brand pitch to ensure that it resonates with your intended audience and leaves a lasting impression.

1 Elevator Pitch

Do you have a 30- to 60-second elevator pitch that summarises who you are, what you do, and why it matters?

Yes ☐ **No** ☐

2 Audience Alignment

Is your pitch tailored to resonate with the specific needs or pain points of your target audience?

Yes ☐ **No** ☐

3 Uniqueness

Does your pitch effectively articulate what sets you apart from others in your field?

Yes ☐ **No** ☐

4 Clarity and Conciseness

Is your pitch easy to understand and free from industry jargon that might confuse the listener?

Yes ☐ **No** ☐

5 Call to Action

Does your pitch include a clear call-to-action that guides the listener on the next steps to engage with you or your brand?

Yes ☐ **No** ☐

6 Versatility

Do you have variations of your pitch for different scenarios or platforms, such as networking events, social media, or formal presentations?

Yes ☐ **No** ☐

7 Visual Aids

If applicable, do you have accompanying visual materials, like slides or a portfolio, that enhance your pitch?

Yes ☐ **No** ☐

8 Rehearsal

Have you practised your pitch multiple times, ideally in front of a trusted colleague or mentor for feedback?

Yes ☐ **No** ☐

9 Live Testing

Have you tested your pitch in real-world scenarios and adjusted it based on the reactions and feedback you received?

Yes ☐ **No** ☐

10 Follow-Up Strategy

Do you have a plan for following up after delivering your pitch to keep the dialogue going?

Yes ☐ **No** ☐

11 Emotional Appeal

Does your pitch connect on an emotional level, establishing trust and rapport?

Yes ☐ **No** ☐

12 Metrics and Results

Does your pitch include specific achievements or metrics that lend credibility to your claims?

Yes ☐ **No** ☐

What I need to do here:

Controversial Branding

Navigating the world of personal branding comes with its own set of challenges, but adding the element of controversy into the mix changes the game entirely. Controversial personal brands often draw attention through provocative opinions, divisive topics, or unconventional practices. While this can generate significant buzz and rapid growth, it also comes with inherent risks, including reputational damage and a polarised audience. This section provides a roadmap for those who find themselves—or aim to be—in this high-risk, high-reward domain.

1 Calculated Risk

Have you consciously adopted a controversial stance, or did it emerge organically? Are you prepared for the potential fallout?

Yes ☐ **No** ☐

2 Ethical Boundaries

While controversy might attract attention, does your brand cross ethical or legal boundaries?

Yes ☐ **No** ☐

3 Target Audience

Is your controversial approach likely to resonate with your target audience, or could it alienate potential supporters?

Yes ☐ **No** ☐

4 Crisis Management

Do you have a plan for managing negative publicity or backlash?

Yes ☐ **No** ☐

5 Consistency

Is the controversial aspect of your brand consistent with your overall mission and values, or does it seem forced and inauthentic?

Yes ☐ **No** ☐

6 Longevity

Have you considered the long-term sustainability of a controversial brand? Is it flexible enough to evolve as social norms change?

Yes ☐ **No** ☐

7 Authenticity

Is your controversial stance accurately representing your beliefs and values, or is it a gimmick to gain attention?

Yes ☐ **No** ☐

8 Engagement

How do you plan to engage with those who disagree with you? Is the goal to provoke or to foster meaningful dialogue with an audience?

Yes ☐ **No** ☐

9 Metrics

What Key Performance Indicators (KPIs) will you use to measure the impact and effectiveness of your controversial branding strategy?

Yes ☐ **No** ☐

10 Reputation

Have you considered how a controversial brand might affect other areas of your life, such as your career, personal relationships, or future endeavours?

Yes ☐ **No** ☐

11 Monetisation

If applicable, do you have a plan for monetising the attention you gain through controversy without compromising your integrity?

Yes ☐ **No** ☐

12 Exit Strategy

Given the volatile nature of controversy, do you have an exit strategy for pivoting or softening your brand if needed?

Yes ☐ **No** ☐

What I need to do here:

Going Viral

In the age of social media, going viral can seem like the Holy Grail of personal branding. A viral moment can catapult you into the spotlight, bring in thousands of new followers, and significantly boost your brand recognition. However, virality is a double-edged sword; it can either make or break your personal brand depending on the content that goes viral and how you handle the attention. This section delves into the nuances of going viral, preparing you for the best and worst outcomes, and offering strategies to sustain the momentum.

1 Readiness

Are you prepared for the attention and scrutiny that comes with going viral? Is your online presence polished and cohesive?

Yes ☐ **No** ☐

2 Relevance

Does the content that went viral align with your brand message and values? If not, how can you redirect the new attention in a way that does?

Yes ☐ **No** ☐

3 Sustainability

How will you maintain interest and engagement levels once the viral buzz has died down?

Yes ☐ **No** ☐

4 Opportunity Maximisation

Are you ready to capitalise on the newfound attention? Think collaborations, interviews, or launching a new product.

Yes ☐ **No** ☐

5 Public Response

How will you manage negative comments or controversies that may arise from the viral content?

Yes ☐ **No** ☐

6 Authenticity

How can you ensure you stay true to your brand's core values and mission in the midst of the hype?

Yes ☐ **No** ☐

7 Measurement

What metrics will you use to assess the impact of going viral on your brand?

Yes ☐ **No** ☐

8 Monetisation

Can you monetise this newfound fame without alienating your existing audience?

Yes ☐ **No** ☐

9 Legacy

How do you want this viral moment to fit into the long-term narrative of your personal brand?

Yes ☐ **No** ☐

10 Crisis Plan

Do you have a crisis management plan in case the content that goes viral is not something you are proud of or misrepresents your brand?

Yes ☐ **No** ☐

11 Adaptability

Are you prepared to evolve your content strategy to incorporate lessons learned from this viral experience?

Yes ☐ **No** ☐

What I need to do here:

Offline Visibility

Your offline visibility is as vital as your online presence in crafting a comprehensive personal brand. Each action contributes to your brand's persona, from networking at industry events to sponsoring causes that align with your values. Utilise business collaterals like brochures to ensure your offline messaging is consistent with your online brand. Consider public appearances and speaking engagements as platforms to showcase your expertise. Join networking groups to both offer and gain value, and don't underestimate the power of word-of-mouth through a robust referral system. Awards, influencer collaborations, and community involvement can further validate your standing in your field. Overall, offline visibility is not just a complement but an integral part of your brand strategy.

1 Physical Networking

Do you attend industry events or meetups?

Yes ☐ **No** ☐

2 Business Collaterals

Are your offline materials like brochures and flyers aligned with your online brand?

Yes ☐ **No** ☐

3 Portfolio

Do you have a physical portfolio that you can present during meetings?

Yes ☐ **No** ☐

4 Public Appearances

Are you making an impact offline through speaking engagements, panels, or workshops?

Yes ☐ No ☐

5 Networking Groups

Are you a member of offline networking groups where you can offer and receive value?

Yes ☐ No ☐

6 Sponsorships

Do you sponsor events or causes aligning with your values?

Yes ☐ No ☐

7 Community Involvement

Are you active in your local or professional community in ways that enhance your personal brand?

Yes ☐ No ☐

8 Influencer Collaborations

Do you collaborate with offline influencers who can vouch for your expertise?

Yes ☐ No ☐

9 Referrals

Do you have a system for encouraging and tracking word-of-mouth referrals?

Yes ☐ No ☐

10 Awards

Do you submit your work for industry awards?

Yes ☐ No ☐

What I need to do here:

Brand Experience

This facet of branding delves into the immediate and lasting impressions you make—from the first encounter with potential clients to fostering long-term relationships. It encompasses everything from the initial interactions on your website or app, characterised by user-friendly UX/UI, to consistent messaging throughout the customer journey. Additionally, brand experience is not just transactional; it's relational. Post-purchase engagement, value-added services, and targeted personalisation are crucial for client retention. Also noteworthy is the role of community-building, as it fosters a shared brand experience among your audience.

1 First Impressions

Have you analysed the initial touchpoints where potential clients come into contact with your brand?

Yes ☐ **No** ☐

2 Customer Journey

Is the experience consistent and aligned with your brand at every step?

Yes ☐ **No** ☐

3 Personalisation

Are you customising experiences based on customer behaviour and preferences?

Yes ☐ **No** ☐

4 UX/UI

Is your website or app user-friendly, and does it offer an exceptional user experience?

Yes ☐ **No** ☐

5 Post-Purchase Experience

Are you nurturing clients even after the transaction is complete?

Yes ☐ **No** ☐

6 Value-Added Services

Do you offer any extras that enhance customer satisfaction, like educational content or loyalty programs?

Yes ☐ **No** ☐

7 Retention Strategies

Do you have a plan for encouraging repeat business?

Yes ☐ **No** ☐

8 Community Building

Are you creating a space for your audience to connect and share experiences?

Yes ☐ **No** ☐

What I need to do here:

Neuroscience & Branding

In an era where personal branding has become more of a necessity than a choice, leveraging the insights of neuroscience can offer a cutting-edge advantage. This section delves into the psychological and neurological elements that affect how your brand is perceived, remembered, and trusted. Drawing upon neuroscience research, we'll explore how human brains are wired to perceive information, make judgments, and establish connections and how this knowledge can be harnessed to elevate your personal brand to a new dimension.

Neuroplasticity tells us that our brains are continually reshaping themselves based on our experiences. When you consistently offer value, your audience's brains can literally rewire to associate your personal brand with positive traits like trustworthiness and expertise. Emotional triggers, particularly those rooted in storytelling, can help forge these neural pathways more robustly than dry, factual presentations ever could.

1 Emotional Engagement

Are you using storytelling or other techniques to tap into your audience's emotions effectively?

Yes ☐ **No** ☐

2 Neural Associations

What words, colours, or symbols are you consistently associating with your brand to forge strong neural pathways in your audience's minds?

Yes ☐ No ☐

3 Mirror Neurons

Are you using video or face-to-face interaction to foster empathy and create a bond by activating mirror neurons?

Yes ☐ No ☐

4 Reward Systems

How are you leveraging your audience's brain reward systems, such as dopamine release, through valuable content or engagement?

Yes ☐ No ☐

5 Cognitive Load

Is your messaging clear and simple enough to be processed and remembered, or is it creating unnecessary cognitive strain?

Yes ☐ No ☐

6 Priming and Anchoring

Are you using these psychological techniques to set your audience up for specific perceptions or reactions?

Yes ☐ No ☐

7 Social Proof

How are you tapping into the brain's natural inclination to trust the wisdom of the crowd?

Yes ☐ No ☐

8 Sensory Perception

Are you leveraging multi-sensory brand experiences to make your brand more memorable?

Yes ☐ No ☐

9 First Impressions

Given that the brain takes as little as seven seconds to form an initial impression, how are you ensuring that the first interaction with your brand is positive?

Yes ☐ No ☐

What I need to do here:

CHAPTER 7

DRIVE

Last but not least, we have the Drive section. Branding isn't a set-it-and-forget-it endeavour; it's a journey. This final phase is dedicated to propelling your brand forward through ongoing marketing strategies, self-development, and performance evaluations. It's the continual fine-tuning and momentum-building that turns good brands into great ones.

Strategic Brand Communication: Action Plan

In the realm of "Strategic Brand Communication," having an action plan isn't just recommended—it's essential. This blueprint encompasses a comprehensive strategy that allocates appropriate resources for effective execution, both online and offline. At its core, the plan targets meaningful engagement with your audience, underpinned by consistent messaging across platforms. It's not just about broadcasting; it's about listening too. Key performance indicators (KPIs) are identified to measure the plan's efficacy, while staff training ensures team alignment with brand values. The built-in review mechanisms and budget outlines facilitate ongoing adjustments. Feedback loops complete the cycle, allowing real-time responsiveness to your audience's needs and preferences.

1 Comprehensive Plan

Do you have a comprehensive strategic brand communication plan documented?

Yes ☐ **No** ☐

2 Resource Allocation

Have you allocated sufficient resources—time, money, and human resources—to implement your plan?

Yes ☐ **No** ☐

3 Brand Showcasing

Does your plan cover all aspects of showcasing your personal brand, including online and offline channels?

Yes ☐ No ☐

4 Audience Impact

Does your plan specifically aim to impact your target audiences in ways that are meaningful to them?

Yes ☐ No ☐

5 Message Consistency

Is there a plan to ensure that your brand messaging will be consistent across various platforms?

Yes ☐ No ☐

6 KPIs and Metrics

Have you identified key performance indicators (KPIs) that will help you gauge and measure the effectiveness of your communication efforts?

Yes ☐ No ☐

7 Staff Training

Have you considered any training or workshops to ensure your team is aligned with your brand communication strategy?

Yes ☐ No ☐

8 Review Mechanism

Is there a regular review process to evaluate the effectiveness of the communication plan and make necessary adjustments?

Yes ☐ No ☐

9 Budget

Does your plan include a detailed budget outline, including potential ROI on specific initiatives?

Yes ☐ No ☐

10 Feedback Loops

Have you set up mechanisms to collect audience feedback and adapt your strategies?

Yes ☐ No ☐

What I need to do here:

Multi-Funnel Approach for Personal Branding

In today's digital landscape, a one-size-fits-all funnel won't suffice. This section explores different types of funnels for your personal brand, each tailored to specific objectives, from building awareness to nurturing relationships. Understanding these multiple funnels can help you create a tailored approach for each audience segment and purpose. Different funnels require different strategies, content, and metrics. By having a multi-funnel approach, you give your personal brand the flexibility and reach to appeal to a diversified audience while fulfilling various objectives. This approach ensures that you capture attention and interest effectively, guide them through the buyer's journey, and establish lasting relationships.

1 Awareness Funnel

Are you using awareness campaigns to generate initial interest and attract a wider audience? What key metrics are you using?

Yes ☐ **No** ☐

2 Engagement Funnel

What strategies and types of content are you using to deepen the relationship with your audience after initial contact?

Yes ☐ **No** ☐

3 Conversion Funnel

How are you guiding interested prospects toward making a commitment, whether that's a purchase or other desired action? What are the KPIs?

Yes ☐ No ☐

4 Retention Funnel

What post-conversion techniques are you using to maintain relationships and encourage repeat business or engagements?

Yes ☐ No ☐

5 Advocacy Funnel

How are you turning satisfied clients or customers into brand advocates who will share and refer others to your brand?

Yes ☐ No ☐

6 Educational Funnel

Are you providing value in the form of educational content to establish thought leadership in your industry?

Yes ☐ No ☐

7 Custom Funnel

Have you identified a need for a specialised funnel unique to your personal brand's objectives or audience?

Yes ☐ No ☐

What I need to do here:

AI and Personal Branding

In the modern branding landscape, artificial intelligence (AI) isn't just an add-on; it's becoming a core component. This section focuses on integrating AI into your personal brand strategy to automate tasks, provide deeper insights, personalise engagement, and even predict future trends. Leveraging AI can significantly elevate your brand's visibility, engagement, and effectiveness. AI can be a significant asset for your personal branding efforts, offering you a range of tools and insights previously accessible only to large corporations. When used wisely, AI can give you the competitive edge you need to excel in a crowded marketplace.

1 Chatbots for Engagement

Are you using AI-powered chatbots to engage visitors on your personal website or social channels and to answer frequently asked questions?

Yes ☐ **No** ☐

2 Predictive Analytics

Are you utilising AI to analyse your brand's data to predict future customer behaviour and trends?

Yes ☐ **No** ☐

3 Content Curation

Do you employ AI tools to automatically curate and share content that is relevant to your target audience?

Yes ☐ **No** ☐

4 Personalisation Algorithms

Are you using AI to personalise email campaigns, website experiences, or social media outreach based on user behaviour and preferences?

Yes ☐ **No** ☐

5 Sentiment Analysis

Do you leverage AI to analyse customer feedback and social mentions to get a sense of the public sentiment around your personal brand?

Yes ☐ **No** ☐

6 SEO Optimisation

Are you using AI tools to optimise your personal website's search engine rankings continually?

Yes ☐ **No** ☐

7 Voice Search and Smart Assistants

Have you optimised your personal brand for voice search, considering the rise of AI-powered smart assistants like Siri, Alexa, and Google Assistant?

Yes ☐ **No** ☐

8 Automated Reporting

Do you use AI to generate real-time analytics reports, giving you actionable insights with minimal effort?

Yes ☐ **No** ☐

9 Influencer Identification

Are you using AI algorithms to identify key influencers and brand advocates in your industry who align with your personal brand?

Yes ☐ **No** ☐

10 Career Path Prediction

For personal growth, are you using AI to predict future career path scenarios and the skills you might need to develop?

Yes ☐ **No** ☐

What I need to do here:

TOP AI tools to Consider

The Top AI Tools for Personal Brands' section guides you through the gamut of AI tools available to upscale your personal brand. Whether it's content creation, analytics, or customer service, AI can offer invaluable support. This section helps you identify which AI tools are not only popular but are also most effective for your unique brand needs. Do note that these tools are changing and evolving rapidly, so even the ones suggested here might be replaced with something better in a relatively short period. As such, keep updating and evolving with these tools.

1 Content Generation

Are you using AI tools like OpenAI's GPT-3 or GPT-4 to enhance your content?

Yes ☐ **No** ☐

2 Social Media Automation

Are you using Buffer or Hootsuite's AI features for scheduling and analytics?

Yes ☐ **No** ☐

3 Sentiment Analysis

Have you tried Brandwatch to gauge public sentiment around your brand?

Yes ☐ **No** ☐

4 SEO Optimisation

Are tools like SEMRUSH, Clearscope or MarketMuse part of your SEO strategy?

Yes ☐ **No** ☐

5 Customer Segmentation

Are you using Optimizely for AI-based audience segmentation?

Yes ☐ **No** ☐

6 Chatbots

Have you considered Drift or Intercom for AI chatbot services on your site?

Yes ☐ **No** ☐

7 Email Marketing

Are you employing Mailchimp's AI features to tailor your email campaigns?

Yes ☐ **No** ☐

8 Data Analytics

Is Google Analytics' AI feature part of your performance assessment?

Yes ☐ **No** ☐

9 Voice Search

Have you optimised for voice search using tools like Dialogflow?

Yes ☐ **No** ☐

10 Translation Services

Are you using DeepL or Google's AutoML Translation?

Yes ☐ **No** ☐

11 Visual Recognition

Is IBM's Watson Visual Recognition tool analysing your visual data?

Yes ☐ **No** ☐

12 Video Analysis

Have you considered Vidyard for performance metrics on your video content?

Yes ☐ **No** ☐

13 Personalisation

Are you using Dynamic Yield for customising digital experiences?

Yes ☐ **No** ☐

14 A/B Testing

Do you use Adobe Target for AI-powered A/B tests?

Yes ☐ **No** ☐

15 Trend Prediction

Are you utilising Crayon for market and competitive intelligence?

Yes ☐ **No** ☐

16 CRM Integration

Is Salesforce Einstein integrated into your CRM system?

Yes ☐ **No** ☐

17 Workflow Automation

Are you using Zapier's AI capabilities to automate repetitive tasks?

Yes ☐ **No** ☐

18 Influencer Matching

Have you tried Upfluence to find the right influencers?

Yes ☐ No ☐

19 Fraud Prevention

Is Darktrace part of your brand's cybersecurity arsenal?

Yes ☐ No ☐

20 Virtual Events

Do you use InEvent for providing tailored experiences in virtual events?

Yes ☐ No ☐

21 Video Editing

Are you using AI-based video editors like Lumen5 or Runway ML for high-quality videos?

Yes ☐ No ☐

22 Image Editing

Do you use AI-enhanced image editors like remove.bg or Canva's design suggestions?

Yes ☐ No ☐

23 Audio Editing

Have you used Descript or Audacity for smart audio editing and transcribing?

Yes ☐ No ☐

24 Interactive Content

Are you using tools like Ceros & TOME for creating interactive content?

Yes ☐ No ☐

What I need to do here:

Online Brand Ecosystem

In today's digitised world, a robust digital presence is non-negotiable for creating a compelling personal brand. Starting with SEO, it's crucial that your brand ranks well in search results, allowing you to reach your target audience effectively. Consistent monitoring of your online reputation can't be overemphasised. Your online assets must not only be mobile-friendly but also deliver an exceptional User Experience (UX). Data-driven decision-making through regular analytics tracking is critical for strategic planning. Social media, often the face of your online persona, should be active and aligned with your overall brand message. If you have an e-commerce element, ensuring it is user-friendly and secure can significantly impact customer trust. Email marketing continues to be a reliable channel for direct communication with your audience. Additionally, quick and efficient online customer service is a must in this age of immediacy. Security protocols, like SSL certificates, are non-negotiable to protect user data. Localisation can offer a personalised touch if you're catering to a global audience. The quality of backlinks and quick load times of your web pages also contribute to your online credibility. Finally, collaborations with digital partners can greatly extend your online reach and influence.

1 SEO

Is your personal brand easily searchable and ranks well on search engines?

Yes ☐ No ☐

2 Online Reputation

Are you monitoring and managing your reputation online?

Yes ☐ No ☐

3 Mobile Optimisation

Are your online assets mobile-friendly?

Yes ☐ No ☐

4 Analytics

Are you regularly tracking and analysing key metrics to assess the reach and engagement of your online assets?

Yes ☐ No ☐

5 Social Media Footprint

Are your social media accounts active, engaging, and aligned with your brand message?

Yes ☐ No ☐

6 E-Commerce

If applicable, is your online store or booking system user-friendly and secure?

Yes ☐ No ☐

7 Email Marketing

Are you leveraging email to maintain a continuous line of communication with your audience?

Yes ☐ No ☐

8 Online Customer Service

Do you have a quick and efficient method for handling online inquiries or complaints?

Yes ☐ No ☐

9 Web Security

Is your website secure, including an SSL certificate, to protect user data?

Yes ☐ No ☐

10 Localisation

Is your content localised to serve different languages or regions if you serve multiple geographic locations?

Yes ☐ No ☐

11 Backlinks

Do you have quality backlinks pointing to your online assets to increase visibility and credibility?

Yes ☐ No ☐

12 Load Time

Do your web pages load quickly to minimise bounce rates?

Yes ☐ No ☐

13 User Experience (UX)

Is the layout and design of your digital platforms intuitive and appealing to users?

Yes ☐ No ☐

14 Digital Partnerships

Have you collaborated with other online platforms or influencers to expand your digital presence?

Yes ☐ No ☐

What I need to do here:

Transparency, Intimacy & Reliability

In the contemporary brand landscape, Transparency, Intimacy, and Reliability aren't just buzzwords; they're the pillars that uphold a strong brand. Transparency isn't merely about being open in business practices; it extends to authenticity in communication and providing a clear window into your product's features and limitations. Intimacy is cultivated by forging an emotional connection with your audience, whether that's through sharing personal stories or behind-the-scenes content. And reliability? It's the bedrock. Consistency in deliverables, prompt responsiveness to inquiries, and showcasing credibility markers like certifications add layers of trust. Facilitating community engagement and prioritising long-term relationship building is essential. Meanwhile, open customer reviews and transparent data handling practices round out a brand's integrity. Accessibility across multiple channels assures your community that you're not just a logo but a dependable entity.

1 Business Practices

Are you open about your business practices and decision-making processes?

Yes ☐ **No** ☐

2 Authenticity

Are you genuine in your communications, avoiding any form of manipulation?

Yes ☐ **No** ☐

3 Consistency

Is there consistency in your quality of work, online posts, and engagement?

Yes ☐ No ☐

4 Responsiveness

Are you responsive to inquiries, feedback, or complaints?

Yes ☐ No ☐

5 Emotional Connection

Are you striving to build an emotional connection with your audience by sharing behind-the-scenes content or personal stories?

Yes ☐ No ☐

6 Product Transparency

Are you open and candid about the features, benefits, and limitations of your products or services?

Yes ☐ No ☐

7 Customer Reviews

Do you encourage and display customer reviews and testimonials, even if they are not all positive?

Yes ☐ No ☐

8 Community Engagement

Are you actively participating in community discussions in a transparent and authentic manner?

Yes ☐ No ☐

9 Privacy

Are you transparent about how you handle and protect customer data?

Yes ☐ No ☐

10 Reliability in Deliverables

Is your brand trustworthy in delivering products or services on time and as promised?

Yes ☐ No ☐

11 Credibility Signals

Do you openly display certifications, accreditations, or other credibility markers?

Yes ☐ No ☐

12 Relationship Building

Do you make an effort to maintain long-term relationships with your community rather than just transactional interactions?

Yes ☐ **No** ☐

13 Accessibility

Is your brand easily reachable through multiple channels for any queries or concerns?

Yes ☐ **No** ☐

What I need to do here:

Corporate Social Responsibility

In an era where transparency and social responsibility are not just buzzwords but imperatives, integrating Corporate Social Responsibility (CSR) into your personal brand can significantly influence public perception and trust. It goes beyond philanthropy and compliance, serving as a mirror reflecting your values and ethical standing. By actively participating in socially responsible initiatives, you contribute to societal betterment and enrich your brand's reputation. This section is designed to guide you in embedding CSR authentically into your personal brand ethos.

1 Alignment

How does your chosen CSR initiative align with your brand values and area of expertise?

Yes ☐ No ☐

2 Authenticity

Is your engagement in CSR activities genuine, or does it appear to be superficial or opportunistic?

Yes ☐ No ☐

3 Communication

How are you communicating your CSR efforts? Is it seamlessly integrated into your overall brand messaging?

Yes ☐ No ☐

4 Community Engagement

Are you engaging your audience and community in your CSR initiatives?

Yes ☐ No ☐

5 Longevity

Is your commitment to CSR a long-term endeavour, or is it a one-off activity?

Yes ☐ No ☐

6 Measurability

How do you measure the impact of your CSR activities?

Yes ☐ No ☐

7 Transparency

Are you open and transparent about your CSR goals and achievements?

Yes ☐ No ☐

8 Community Engagement

Are you actively participating in community discussions in a transparent and authentic manner?

Yes ☐ No ☐

What I need to do here:

Brand Performance Monitoring and Analytics

In today's dynamic marketplace, monitoring your brand's performance isn't a luxury—it's a necessity. The 'Brand Performance Monitoring and Analytics' section aims to encapsulate the multi-faceted dimensions of brand analytics. From tracking digital footprints through website analytics and social media metrics to understanding customer behaviour via feedback and lifetime value assessments, this section provides an exhaustive list of questions to evaluate your brand's health. Furthermore, it encourages brands to look beyond online activities, factoring in offline metrics and market positioning against competitors. All these components coalesce to offer a holistic view of your brand's current standing and future potential.

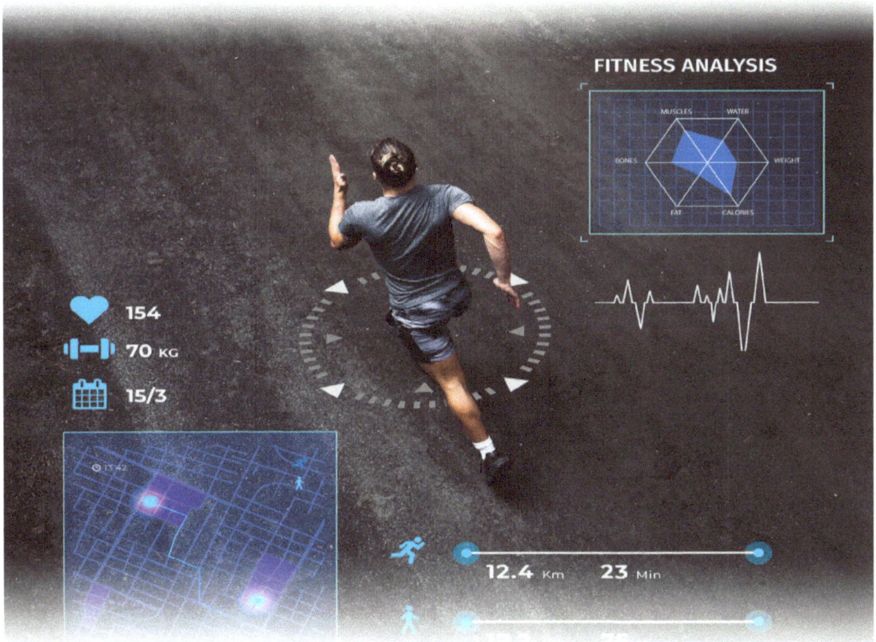

1 Website Analytics

Are you not just tracking visits but also interpreting web analytics to inform business decisions?

Yes ☐ **No** ☐

2 Social Media Metrics

Are you capturing a full range of metrics—likes, shares, follows, and engagement rates—to understand social impact?

Yes ☐ **No** ☐

3 Email List Growth

Are you acquiring, segmenting, and engaging new subscribers?

Yes ☐ **No** ☐

4 Customer Feedback

Are you systematically gathering, analysing, and acting on customer feedback?

Yes ☐ **No** ☐

5 Competitive Analysis

Are you maintaining an up-to-date SWOT analysis to stay ahead of competitors?

Yes ☐ **No** ☐

6 Conversion Rate

Are you identifying bottlenecks in the user journey that affect conversion rates?

Yes ☐ **No** ☐

7 Customer Lifetime Value (CLV)

Have you deployed strategies to maximise CLV?

Yes ☐ **No** ☐

8 ROI Measurements

Are you quantifying the ROI for each marketing channel you invest in?

Yes ☐ **No** ☐

9 Bounce Rate

Are you implementing UX/UI changes based on bounce rate analytics?

Yes ☐ **No** ☐

10 Net Promoter Score (NPS)

Are you using NPS data to improve customer satisfaction and loyalty?

Yes ☐ No ☐

11 Retention Rate

Are you employing tactics to enhance customer retention over specific time intervals?

Yes ☐ No ☐

12 Churn Rate

Are you analysing the reasons behind customer churn to inform retention strategies?

Yes ☐ No ☐

13 Cost Per Acquisition (CPA)

Are you optimising your marketing spend based on CPA?

Yes ☐ No ☐

14 Search Engine Rankings

Are you continuously optimising for search engine algorithm updates?

Yes ☐ No ☐

15 Influencer Metrics

Are you evaluating the effectiveness of influencer collaborations using KPIs?

Yes ☐ No ☐

16 Social Listening

Are you leveraging tools to analyse brand mentions and consumer sentiment across various platforms?

Yes ☐ No ☐

17 Market Share

Are you keeping tabs on your market share and setting targets for growth?

Yes ☐ No ☐

18 Customer Segmentation Analysis

Have you used data analytics for audience segmentation to refine your marketing strategies?

Yes ☐ No ☐

19 Content Engagement

Are you measuring content metrics like dwell time, click-through rate, and social shares?

Yes ☐ **No** ☐

20 Offline Metrics

Are you incorporating metrics from offline sources such as customer feedback, observational data, and one-on-one interviews into your evaluation?

Yes ☐ **No** ☐

What I need to do here:

Professional & Personal Development

In a landscape that's ever-changing, the growth of your personal brand is intrinsically tied to your professional and personal development. The 'Professional & Personal Development' section serves as a reflective roadmap that prompts you to consistently evaluate and elevate your skills, knowledge, and industry engagement. Whether embracing lifelong learning, acquiring relevant certifications, or mastering soft and hard skills, this section aims to be your guide. The section also emphasises the value of mentorship, adaptability, and resilience—cornerstones for building a formidable and versatile personal brand that not just survives but thrives in the marketplace.

1 Skill Assessment

Have you conducted a SWOT analysis to identify gaps in your skills?

Yes ☐ No ☐

2 Continued Learning

Are you engaged in ongoing educational activities, such as workshops, webinars, or online courses?

Yes ☐ No ☐

3 Industry Trends

Are you not only aware of but also leveraging current industry trends to your advantage?

Yes ☐ No ☐

4 Certifications

Have you considered obtaining certifications that could strategically enhance your professional brand?

Yes ☐ No ☐

5 Mentorship

Do you have a structured mentor-mentee relationship that adds reciprocal value?

Yes ☐ No ☐

6 Soft Skills

Are you nurturing emotional intelligence alongside skills like communication and leadership?

Yes ☐ No ☐

7 Hard Skills

Are you taking courses or participating in training to stay current with essential industry-specific technical skills?

Yes ☐ No ☐

8 Adaptability

How robust is your contingency planning for unexpected market changes or personal setbacks?

Yes ☐ No ☐

9 Delegation

Are you employing smart delegation strategies, ensuring you focus on tasks that directly contribute to your personal brand?

Yes ☐ No ☐

10 Resilience

Do you have coping mechanisms in place to recover from professional or personal setbacks?

Yes ☐ No ☐

What I need to do here:

Financial & Legal Brand Assessment

The 'Financial & Legal Brand Assessment' section is a critical cornerstone for anyone serious about growing a resilient and scalable personal brand. This area focuses on the economic and legal factors, often the bedrock of a sustainable brand. From diversifying revenue streams and smart budgeting to setting and regularly reviewing financial goals, this section is designed to keep your fiscal health in peak condition. Moreover, it emphasises the importance of safeguarding your brand's intellectual property through trademarks and being transparent and compliant with legal requirements such as privacy policies. Navigating this dual roadmap will not only protect but also empower your brand's growth trajectory.

1 Revenue Streams

Are your revenue streams diversified, and have you considered potential new avenues?

Yes ☐ No ☐

2 Expenses

Are you employing cost-effective strategies and regularly auditing your expenditures?

Yes ☐ No ☐

3 Financial Goals

Have you set both short-term and long-term financial goals, and are they subject to periodic review?

Yes ☐ No ☐

4 Investments

Are you allocating resources to enhance your brand, such as marketing, quality improvements, or R&D?

Yes ☐ No ☐

5 Pricing Strategy

Have you conducted a thorough market analysis to ensure your pricing is both competitive and profitable?

Yes ☐ No ☐

6 Trademark

Have you secured the necessary trademarks for your brand name, logo, and any other unique brand identifiers?

Yes ☐ No ☐

7 Privacy Policy

Is your privacy policy compliant with legal standards and transparent and easily accessible to your audience?

Yes ☐ No ☐

8 Contracts & Agreements

Are all business dealings and partnerships formalised through legally binding contracts?

Yes ☐ No ☐

9 Risk Assessment

Have you evaluated financial and legal risks, and do you have strategies to mitigate them?

Yes ☐ No ☐

10 Intellectual Property

Are you protecting proprietary methodologies or technologies beyond trademarks?

Yes ☐ No ☐

What I need to do here:

Work-Life Balance

The 'Work-Life Balance' section is integral for anyone growing a personal brand. As much as brand building demands time and effort, it's crucial to allocate space for personal wellness, relationships, and downtime. This section prompts you to scrutinise how effectively you're balancing the professional and the personal. From time management and burnout prevention to the holistic well-being of yourself and your loved ones, the questions aim to ensure that your brand's growth doesn't come at the expense of your life's other valuable facets.

1 Time Management

Are you leveraging time management tools or techniques to balance your professional commitments with your personal life?

Yes ☐ **No** ☐

2 Burnout Check

Do you have specific strategies or routines in place to prevent emotional or physical burnout?

Yes ☐ **No** ☐

3 Health and Wellness

Are you maintaining a consistent exercise regimen, and are you mindful of your nutritional intake?

Yes ☐ **No** ☐

4 Family and Relationships

Are your family relationships and friendships being positively or negatively impacted by the demands of your personal brand?

Yes ☐ **No** ☐

5 Hobbies and Interests

Are you setting aside time for activities outside of work that bring you happiness and relaxation?

Yes ☐ **No** ☐

6 Mental Health

Are you employing mindfulness or other practices to ensure mental well-being?

Yes ☐ **No** ☐

7 Vacation and Downtime

Do you regularly schedule breaks or holidays to recharge?

Yes ☐ **No** ☐

8 Professional Boundaries

Have you set limits on work hours to ensure quality personal time?

Yes ☐ **No** ☐

What I need to do here:

Global Reach

In today's interconnected world, extending your personal brand's impact on a global scale is more feasible than ever. The "Global Reach" section explores critical elements that are essential for successfully taking your brand international, including language localisation, cultural sensitivity, global networking, and understanding of international laws and trends.

1 Language and Localisation

Is your website and content available in multiple languages to cater to a global audience?

Yes ☐ **No** ☐

2 Cultural Sensitivity

Are you ensuring your brand messaging is globally inclusive? Have you conducted research to understand various cultural nuances and taboos?

Yes ☐ **No** ☐

3 Global Networking

Are you a part of international industry organisations or online communities? Do you attend international conferences or webinars to expand your network?

Yes ☐ **No** ☐

4 Legal Considerations

Have you consulted with international legal advisors to ensure your brand complies with regulations in other countries? Are you aware of differing privacy laws and consumer rights worldwide?

Yes ☐ **No** ☐

5 Global Trends

Are you keeping track of international market trends and consumer behaviours that might influence your brand? Do you adjust your brand strategies based on global trends?

Yes ☐ **No** ☐

What I need to do here:

Brand Innovation and Brand Adaptability

In an ever-changing landscape, the ability to innovate and adapt is not just an asset but a necessity for personal brands. The "Brand Innovation and Brand Adaptability" section aims to gauge your readiness for change and your capacity to innovate. This includes harnessing technology, anticipating industry trends, preparing for crises, evolving your brand when necessary, and maintaining a creative approach.

1 Technology Use

Are you employing the latest digital tools and platforms to streamline operations and improve your brand's visibility?

Yes ☐ **No** ☐

2 Future Trends

Do you conduct regular research or consult industry experts to stay abreast of upcoming shifts that could impact your brand?

Yes ☐ **No** ☐

3 Crisis Management

Do you have a well-documented plan and a crisis communication strategy to manage potential brand-threatening situations?

Yes ☐ **No** ☐

4 Brand Evolution

Are you open to iterative rebranding or brand evolution based on market feedback and changing circumstances?

Yes ☐ **No** ☐

5 Creativity

Do you regularly engage in brainstorming sessions, either solo or with your team, to think of innovative ways to elevate your brand?

Yes ☐ **No** ☐

What I need to do here:

Brand Extensions

Expanding your personal brand often involves stepping into new verticals or collaborating with other entities. The "Brand Extensions" section is designed to help you evaluate whether these brand-boosting strategies effectively align with your core brand values and objectives. Assess your product offerings, consider the impact of sub-brands, scrutinise merchandise quality, and vet sponsorships and endorsements to ensure cohesive brand messaging.

1 Products/Services

Do your new offerings strengthen your brand promise and meet your audience's expectations?

Yes ☐ **No** ☐

2 Sub-brands or Sister Brands

Are these aligned so that they either complement or elevate your primary brand rather than confuse or dilute it?

Yes ☐ **No** ☐

3 Merchandising

Is your merchandise not just high-quality but also in sync with your brand's image and values?

Yes ☐ **No** ☐

4 Sponsorships and Endorsements

Do they mesh well with your brand's identity, and are they likely to resonate with your target audience?

Yes ☐ **No** ☐

5 Affiliate Marketing

Are your affiliate partnerships carefully chosen to align with your brand ethos and provide tangible value to your audience?

Yes ☐ **No** ☐

What I need to do here:

Retrospective and Future Planning

The Retrospective and Future Planning section serves as a pivotal checkpoint to gauge the performance of your personal brand over time. It encourages you to reflect on past goals and set actionable objectives for the future. This is the juncture where you rigorously examine your personal brand's current state, drawing on insights to navigate future strategies effectively.

1 Past Goals Review

How well did you meet your past objectives, and what were the key learnings?

Yes ☐ **No** ☐

2 Future Goals Setting

Are your upcoming goals not only SMART but also aligned with your evolving brand strategy?

Yes ☐ **No** ☐

3 SWOT Analysis

Have you recently updated your evaluation of Strengths, Weaknesses, Opportunities, and Threats in the context of market dynamics?

Yes ☐ **No** ☐

4 Action Plans

Have you established specific, step-by-step plans to address identified weaknesses and capitalise on opportunities?

Yes ☐ **No** ☐

5 Periodic Review

How frequently are you performing a comprehensive brand audit to monitor progress and make adjustments?

Yes ☐ **No** ☐

6 Milestone Assessment

Are you marking and celebrating small wins as you reach predefined milestones?

Yes ☐ No ☐

7 Budget Alignment

Are your future plans in line with your financial forecasts and budget?

Yes ☐ No ☐

8 Resource Inventory

Do you have or plan to have the necessary resources (time, talent, capital) to achieve your future goals?

Yes ☐ No ☐

What I need to do here:

Exit Strategies and Succession Planning

Exit Strategies and Succession Planning are critical yet often overlooked elements in personal brand development. Preparing for your brand's eventual transition or closure is not just prudent but essential for sustained value creation. This section prompts you to consider how your brand would evolve without you, ensuring a lasting impact and smooth handover.

1 Exit Strategy

Have you outlined a comprehensive plan detailing how you aim to exit or evolve your brand in the future?

Yes ☐ No ☐

2 Legacy Planning

Beyond memory, what tangible impacts do you want your brand to leave behind?

Yes ☐ No ☐

3 Asset Allocation

In your absence, how would the assets of your brand be managed or divided?

Yes ☐ No ☐

4 Business Continuity

Have you identified and trained successors who can run your brand effectively without you?

Yes ☐ No ☐

5 Documenting Processes

Are all workflows, best practices, and processes comprehensively documented to facilitate a smooth transition?

Yes ☐ No ☐

6 Stakeholder Communication

Is there a plan to inform clients, partners, and stakeholders about changes in leadership or brand direction?

Yes ☐ No ☐

7 Financial Liabilities

Are there plans in place to settle all financial obligations as part of your exit strategy?

Yes ☐ No ☐

8 Intellectual Property

What will happen to your brand's intellectual property, and how will it be managed post-exit?

Yes ☐ No ☐

What I need to do here:

Brand Crisis Communication

The capacity to manage crises effectively is a vital facet of any resilient personal brand. Crisis moments can either break your brand or be an opportunity for growth, depending on your preparation and response. This section explores your readiness to communicate transparently and effectively in crisis situations and your strategies for regaining public trust post-crisis.

1 Crisis Communication Plan

Do you have a detailed crisis communication strategy that delineates roles, responsibilities, and action steps?

Yes ☐ No ☐

2 Message Control

Do you have predefined messages or templates that can be quickly customised and communicated during a crisis?

Yes ☐ No ☐

3 Spokesperson

Who is authorised to speak on behalf of your brand in a crisis, and are they trained for it?

Yes ☐ No ☐

4 Media Channels

What media channels will you use for crisis communication to ensure effective reach?

Yes ☐ No ☐

5 Post-Crisis Review

Do you have a plan for post-crisis assessment to understand what worked and what didn't?

Yes ☐ No ☐

6 Rebuilding Trust

How robust is your post-crisis strategy for re-establishing credibility and trust?

Yes ☐ No ☐

7 Prevention

Are there preventive measures in place to avoid similar crises in the future?

Yes ☐ No ☐

8 Transparency

How will you ensure transparent communication with stakeholders during and after the crisis?

Yes ☐ No ☐

9 Customer Engagement

Do you have a plan to manage customer queries and concerns during the crisis?

Yes ☐ **No** ☐

10 Legal Considerations

Are you prepared to handle any legal repercussions that may arise from the crisis?

Yes ☐ **No** ☐

What I need to do here:

CHAPTER 8

YOUR PERSONAL BRAND REVIEW & ACTION PLAN FRAMEWORK

After going through the 5 Phases of personal branding—**Discover, Define, Develop, Deliver, and Drive**—you've likely accumulated valuable insights about your brand. It's time to consolidate these insights and translate them into concrete action items. From here you can also set key goals for your brand.

DISCOVER

List the top 3 insights you've gained about your personal brand's current state.

INSIGHT 1 :	
INSIGHT 2 :	
INSIGHT 3 :	

Action Items :	
Short-Term Goals (1-3 months) :	
Medium-Term Goals (4-12 months) :	
Long-Term Goals (1-3 years) :	

DEFINE

What are the key elements you've defined for your brand?

INSIGHT 1 :	
INSIGHT 2 :	
INSIGHT 3 :	

Action Items :	
Short-Term Goals (1-3 months) :	
Medium-Term Goals (4-12 months) :	
Long-Term Goals (1-3 years) :	

DEVELOP

What strategies and differentiators have you decided on?

INSIGHT 1 :	
INSIGHT 2 :	
INSIGHT 3 :	

Action Items :	
Short-Term Goals (1-3 months) :	
Medium-Term Goals (4-12 months) :	
Long-Term Goals (1-3 years) :	

DELIVER

What are the key elements you've defined for your brand?

INSIGHT 1 :	
INSIGHT 2 :	
INSIGHT 3 :	

Action Items :	
Short-Term Goals (1-3 months) :	
Medium-Term Goals (4-12 months) :	
Long-Term Goals (1-3 years) :	

DRIVE

Summarise your plan for sustaining and enhancing brand performance.

INSIGHT 1 :	
INSIGHT 2 :	
INSIGHT 3 :	

Action Items :	
Short-Term Goals (1-3 months) :	
Medium-Term Goals (4-12 months) :	
Long-Term Goals (1-3 years) :	

This framework is designed to be a living document. As you accomplish goals and tackle action items, revisit and update the plan. It will serve as a dynamic tool to keep you focused and guide you as you elevate your personal brand to new heights.

CHAPTER 9

CONCLUSION

Congratulations, you've navigated the labyrinthine personal branding journey using a map uniquely engineered for success— **"Ultimate Personal Branding Checklist."** This checklist isn't just a static document; it's a dynamic tool designed to evolve with you as you manoeuvre through the ever-changing landscape of personal branding.

By meticulously traversing through the five pivotal phases—**Discover, Define, Develop, Deliver, and Drive**—you've empowered yourself with invaluable insights into the DNA of your brand. Now, you're not just reacting to the branding ecosystem around you; you're proactively shaping it, too.

The Checklist as Your Brand's Lifeline

The checklist serves as a lifeline for your personal brand. Whether you're launching a new venture, pivoting your career, or scaling up existing efforts, you'll find reasons aplenty to revisit it. You may be looking to diversify revenue streams, or you may need to re-evaluate your brand's global reach amid shifting geopolitical landscapes. Your reasons can be as varied as they are specific to your circumstances.

The Art and Science of Using the Checklist

Using this checklist is both an art and a science. It offers a rigorous framework for logical assessment through our defined phases and carefully chosen questions. Yet, the 'how' of acting on these insights—turning gaps into opportunities and strengths into unique selling propositions—calls for creativity and intuition. And for that, you don't just need to master the checklist; you also need to master yourself.

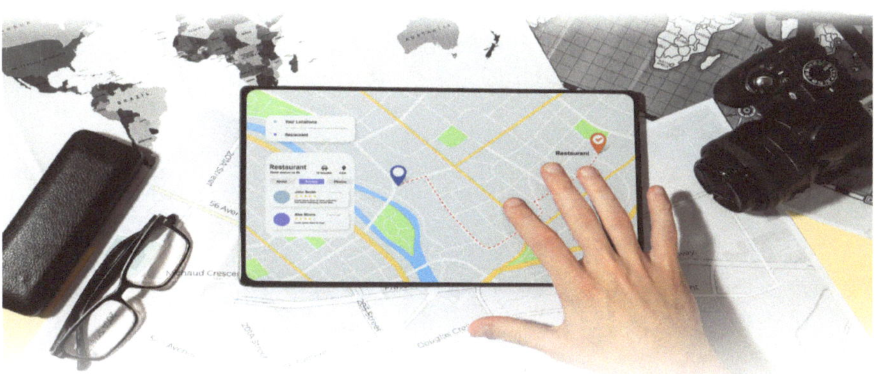

A Lifetime of Brand Evolution

Throughout my 27 years of coaching personal brands around the globe, I've witnessed first-hand the power of systematic evaluation and strategic action. Some of my most rewarding experiences have been watching clients climb up the rungs of brand maturity. You, too, will undergo a similar evolution as you cycle through this checklist repeatedly, updating your action plans and reconfiguring your strategies.

Your Next Steps and Beyond

With the aid of the Personal Brand Review & Action Plan Framework, you can funnel your insights into a succinct action plan. The true test of your brand's resilience and adaptability comes when these plans are implemented. Remember, planning is essential, but execution is paramount. Accountability is key here; whether it's a trusted mentor, a dedicated team, or sophisticated tracking software, make sure you have mechanisms in place to monitor your progress and make course corrections as needed.

The Dynamic Nature of Branding

Branding is not a one-time activity but an ongoing process. The dynamism of today's world—with its technological advances, cultural shifts, and market fluctuations—demands a brand that is both stable in its core values and flexible in its expression. The ability to balance consistency with adaptability will set you apart in a saturated marketplace.

Your Brand is Your Legacy

As you move forward, remember that your personal brand is more than just a tool for career growth or business success. It's your legacy. Your brand is an evolving story of who you are, the value you provide, and the impact you make. Make that story an extraordinary one.

In conclusion, armed with this checklist and the resolve to implement it, you're no longer just a player in the game of personal branding; you're a formidable contender. So, take control today and lead your brand toward the impact, authenticity, and success you've always envisioned. Your future self will thank you.

ABOUT DR. JEROME JOSEPH

Dr Jerome Joseph, CSP, GSF, HoF, ranked No. 2 in the world as a Global Brand Guru in 2022, is a best-selling author & recognised thought leader. Through Speaking, Coaching and Consulting, he collaborates with clients worldwide to drive impactful transformations in Brand Strategy, Brand Experience, Internal Branding, Personal Branding and Branded Customer Experience.

With his past experiences as a CEO & Board Member of a publicly-listed brand agency & group, Dr. Jerome brings real-life brand expertise through his speaking, coaching and consulting arms. He is a best-selling Author of 9 books on branding and has over 27 years of experience working with over 1000 brands, including numerous notable Fortune 500 companies, in 37 countries.

The combination of real-life consulting experience with these Fortune 500 companies, global expertise, and proven speaking skills makes Dr. Jerome a sought-after speaker and consultant in global markets.

Key achievements:

- Certified Speaking Professional (CSP)- designation for speaking excellence which is held only by the top 12% speakers in the world

- Global Speaking Fellow (GSF)- designation for excellence in global speaking. He is the 2nd Singaporean to achieve this award and the 30th speaker worldwide to do the same. Currently, less than 1% of speakers globally have this designation.

- Practising Management Consultant (PMC)- exclusive consulting designation for industry veterans

- 2020 and 2022- No.2 Global Brand Thought Leader in the World

- Asia Speaker Hall of Fame (HoF) - Youngest Inductee for Lifetime achievements and expertise in professional speaking in Asia.

- Doctoral Thesis on the Impact of Brand and Culture Transformation within Organisations

ABOUT DR. JEROME JOSEPH

Dr Jerome Joseph is a Speaker, Coach, and Consultant across the pillars of Brand Strategy, Digital Branding, Motivation, Branded Cultures, Personal Branding and Branded Customer Experience. Here is a snapshot of his popular Signature Programs:

BRAND STRATEGY

- The Brand Playbook: Game Changing Strategies and Ideas to Win in the Marketplace
- Experience Branding: Establish Deep Audience Connection Through Our Brand Experience Framework
- Lessons From The Legends: Asia or Global
- Brand Mastery in the Digital Age
- Once Upon A Brand: The Power Of Brand Story Telling

DIGITAL BRANDING

- Branding 5.0: New Media, New Conversations, New Experiences
- Digital Branding: Unleash your Brand Online
- Branding and AI: Let's Do This
- Turn Me On: Content Marketing Masterclass

MOTIVATION

- Your Brand Legacy: Creating A Brand that you are remembered for

BRANDED CULTURES

- Internal Branding: Growing Your Brand From Within
- The Brand Champion Mindset
- Brand Leadership: Creating Leaders Led by Brand Purpose

PERSONAL BRANDING

- TURN Me ON: Strategies To Build Your Personal Brand
- Branded Social Selling: The Power of Personal Branding to Drive Sales

BRANDED CUSTOMER EXPERIENCE

- Branded Customer Experience: Staging ExtraOrdinary Branded Experiences
- Brand Loyalty: How To Transform Customers To Raving Fans

Other Books written by **Dr Jerome Joseph:**

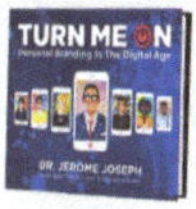

Turn Me On: Personal Branding In The Digital Age

The Brand Playbook: 88 Game Changing Strategies and Ideas to Win in The Marketplace

Internal Branding: Growing Your Brand From Within

Get Aligned! 10 Principles to Grow Your Internal Brand

Stand Out: 30 Principles to Grow Your Personal Brand

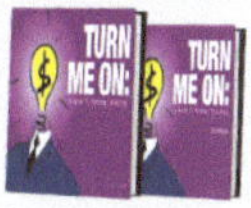

Turn Me On: A Guide To Personal Branding [Book & Workbook]

The Brand Theatre: Staging Extraordinary Branded Customer Experiences [Book & Workbook]

www.ingramcontent.com/pod-product-compliance
Lightning Source LLC
LaVergne TN
LVHW051128210926
848482LV00001B/22
* 9 7 9 8 8 9 2 3 3 9 2 3 0 *